Letters *with* Smokie

Letters *with* Smokie

Blindness and More-Than-Human Relations

Rod Michalko *and* Dan Goodley
with Smokie

UNIVERSITY OF MANITOBA PRESS

Letters with Smokie: Blindness and More-than-Human Relations
© Rod Michalko and Dan Goodley 2023

27 26 25 24 23   1 2 3 4 5

University of Manitoba Press
Winnipeg, Manitoba, Canada
Treaty 1 Territory
uofmpress.ca

Cataloguing data available from Library and Archives Canada
ISBN 978-1-77284-033-9 (PAPER)
ISBN 978-1-77284-035-3 (PDF)
ISBN 978-1-77284-036-0 (EPUB)
ISBN 978-1-77284-034-6 (BOUND)

Cover and interior illustration by James Culleton
Cover design by Kirk Warren
Interior design by Jess Koroscil

The lyrics from "Revolution," words and music by John Lennon and Paul McCartney, copyright © 1968 Sony Music Publishing (US) LLC, are reprinted with the permission of Hal Leonard LLC.

The lyrics from "Two of Us," words and music by John Lennon and Paul McCartney, copyright © 1969, 1970 Sony Music Publishing (US) LLC, are reprinted with the permission of Hal Leonard LLC.

The lyrics from "The Pilgrim: Chapter 33," words and music by Kris Kristofferson, copyright © 1970 Resaca Music Publishing Co., are reprinted with the permission of Hal Leonard LLC.

All rights administered by Sony Music Publishing (US) LLC, 424 Church Street, Suite 1200, Nashville, TN 37219. International copyright secured. All rights reserved.

The University of Manitoba Press acknowledges the financial support for its publication program provided by the Government of Canada through the Canada Book Fund, the Canada Council for the Arts, the Manitoba Department of Sport, Culture, and Heritage, the Manitoba Arts Council, and the Manitoba Book Publishing Tax Credit.

Funded by the Government of Canada   Canadä

For
guides everywhere

Contents

Introduction

Rod Michalko

To say that Smokie inspired the writing of this book is an understatement, for without his influence it never would have been written. Smokie came into my life in 1992. He was a big, strong, fast black Labrador retriever and, in addition to that, he was my guide dog. My partner, Tanya Titchkosky, and I were living in Toronto with our two cats, Jessie and Sugar, shortly before Smokie came into our lives. This was a crucial time of my life. My vision was beginning to change . . . radically.

I had been legally blind since my late childhood/early teens. I had always been able to make my way through the world with relative ease. Things were changing though. I began to experience a great deal of difficulty in getting around and finally reached the point where I gave in to using the white cane. I reasoned that the white cane would not only assist me in getting around relatively safely, it would also indicate to others that I was blind. This reasoning quickly lost its reason.

I had been involved in athletics for most of my life. I gravitated to team sports such as football and basketball both because I enjoyed them and because footballs and basketballs were relatively big and easier for me to see. I also ran track, did gymnastics, and weight trained. These athletic activities gave me a certain grace of movement even though I was legally blind. I treasured this movement but, like my vision, it too changed . . . radically.

While the white cane did give me a level of safety and did let others know of my blindness, it did nothing to preserve even a modicum of grace in my movement. It was a slow and clunky way of making my way through the world. I attributed this clunkiness to my blindness. There are many blind people, some of whom I know, who use the white cane with competence and grace. I wasn't one of them. It just didn't work for me.

It was Tanya that first raised the possibility of a guide dog. After some initial reluctance, I agreed to at least investigate the possibility. Following many discussions and much research on guide dogs and guide dog schools, I found myself in a guide dog training facility, just outside of Toronto in Oakville, about to embark on a one-month residential training program to acquire a guide dog.

Then, Smokie. And things changed . . . very radically.

To this day, I still remember the trainer bringing Smokie to my room at the guide dog school; this is when I knew Smokie and I were a team. To quote previous writing about this experience:

> The trainer called out from outside my door, "I'm here with your dog." I heard the door open and the words, "Here's Smokie." . . .
> The trainer left us alone, and we spent the next hour playing with the toys I had purchased for

him. I showed him his bed, his food bowl, and the desk drawer where I was storing his treats. Smokie was especially interested in the last, and for the next month he went directly to the desk drawer whenever we returned to our room. We spent the last half hour of our first morning together on the floor, me sitting and Smokie sleeping, his head resting on my lap. At noon, I put his harness on and we proceeded first to his relief area and then to the lunch room. This was the first of countless times that I put the harness on *my* guide. I flexed my fingers gently around the harness handle and leash, and in the speaking of the very first "forward" to Smokie, I knew that my search for a guide was over and that Smokie and I would travel the world together for a very long time to come.[1]

The month-long training program was intense, but not without its fun. Smokie was highly trained for guide work. I wasn't. The first two weeks were spent getting to a level of competence where I could at least begin to allow Smokie to guide me; the last two weeks were devoted to honing our skills. What was most fun was getting to know Smokie. He and I got to know each other during that month, figuring out our likes, dislikes, what made us happy. The month was more than enough time for us to grow very close, to bond, as the trainers put it.

A noticeable difference in my movement happened almost immediately as I learned how to work with Smokie.

My movements had already started to take on a Smokie-like grace when he and I left the training school and moved home. This is where my movement into blindness with Smokie as my guide took me into a world I never thought possible.

I spoke of this movement into blindness with Smokie in my book *The Two in One: Walking with Smokie, Walking with Blindness*. In it, I describe in detail getting to know Smokie and working with him at the guide dog training school. I spoke, too, of moving home and of becoming even closer to Smokie and of learning the nuances of working with him as he guided me through the world and into a new experience of blindness.

In the summer of 1997, Tanya and I packed up our belongings. Along with Smokie, Cassis, Tanya's black Labrador, and our two cats, we piled into a van and two of our friends drove us to Antigonish, Nova Scotia, where we embarked on nine years of teaching in the Department of Sociology at St. Francis Xavier University. I also speak of this experience in *Two in One*.

On 4 June 2001, Smokie passed away following a brief struggle with liver cancer. We remained in Antigonish until 2006, when we moved back to Toronto. During this time Cassis passed away and so did Jessie and Sugar. Tanya and I moved back to Toronto, alone . . . with our memories.

What follows may be read as reflections on my life with Smokie after his passing. His influence on me and my experience of blindness remains as strong now as it was when he was alive. While *The Two in One* was written in my voice, this book is written in what I have come to know as Smokie's voice. I tried to imagine how he would interpret and understand some of what I wrote in *The Two in One* and what he might think of my life since his passing. This book, then, is one of imagination. It asks how different perspectives, ones that can be reached only through imagination, influence us. In particular, this book asks us to imagine the perspectives of blindness and of non-human animals, and asks us to imagine even sight as a perspective.

This project, I came to realize, had been years in the making. It marks a thirty-year and counting relationship I have with Smokie—ten years when he was alive and we were "together-together," as he and I think of it, and twenty years since his passing. As I said earlier, we spent the first five years of our life together-together in Toronto and the remaining years in Antigonish. Since Smokie's passing, Tanya and I returned to Toronto, where we continue our work in disability studies at the University of Toronto. I retired from the university a few years ago and continue my work at a more leisurely pace.

My work in disability studies has changed in recent years. It engages less and less with disability in general and focuses, not in an ocular-centric way, more directly on blindness. Smokie's continuing influence on my life and work has not only grown, it has sharpened and intensified, and it seems to have done so as though in sync with my "refocus" on blindness. He has been with me in this refocus, a move which has proven to be not only intriguing and mysterious, but adventuresome as well.

As I was beginning to embark on this new path, I met Dan Goodley, a disability studies scholar from the UK. Like the new path, my ever-growing relationship with Dan was full of wonder, mystery, and adventure. He is, without question, one of my best friends. More than that, Tanya and I have become very close friends not only with Dan but with his partner, Rebecca Lawthom, head of the School of Education at the

University of Sheffield, and their two daughters, Ruby and Rosa. We have come to characterize our friendship as family. It is within the context of my life with Tanya, with our life with our UK family and, especially within the context of my relationship with Smokie, both when he was alive and now, that the idea for this book took shape. My decades of intense experience with blindness and with its travelling companion, sight, provide the backdrop for this project and are also responsible for its completion.

This project began in a concrete way, albeit unintentionally, in late 2020 in the midst of the COVID-19 pandemic. Tanya and I had just received a copy of Dan's new book, *Disability and Other Human Questions,* and I was writing an email of congratulations to him. As I was writing the email, I suddenly began to wonder what the term "other human questions" might mean to Smokie, particularly in relation to his experience of blindness, an experience he had for most of his life. Along with being a loving friend and dedicated guide, Smokie was also confident and independent, and had a strong sense of how he ought to guide me, not only through blindness but into it as well. It was as though he dedicated himself to showing me a blindness in which we could both live creatively and with pride.

I gave my imagination free rein and, along with my congratulations, I added some opinions from Smokie, in the way I imagined him speaking them. Pressing the key that would send the email hurtling through some only imagined virtual space to end up on Dan's computer screen in West Yorkshire, I smiled and whispered, "Yes. Smokie would have said this." There is of course the tricky, inescapable process of anthropomorphizing Smokie as I write these letters to Dan, not to mention the tricky process of channelling. After all, I am writing them on his behalf and in a voice that he did not have. Moreover, I am involving Smokie in an activity that is strictly the province of human animals, namely, letter writing. There is no other way to frame what follows other than the anthropomorphization of Smokie. And yet, I am certain that the following letters are more than merely an anthropomorphized facsimile of his voice; they are also letters that Smokie would have penned . . . if he could have. The certainty of this claim flows from our life, from the life that Smokie and I lived and continue to live. Our life together showed me with equal certainty that Smokie had moved beyond any conventional human understanding of animal life and that I had moved beyond any conventional human understanding of human life. The two of us blended the "nature" of animal life and the "social" of human life to generate an estranged-familiarity; hence the main title of my book on our life together, *The Two in One*. Throughout our life together, I spoke with Smokie in human terms; I gave him instructions both verbally and with gestures when he guided me, and spoke with him constantly and nearly continuously as we moved through our world together. Smokie, in turn, spoke with me with his voice—what he told me through his guide-dog harness, his ever-changing pace, and, of course, through barks and other sounds. Soon after we began our life together, I was able to understand the different meanings of the variety of these barks and sounds. He spoke with me, too, through his body, through a series of touches, nudges, and, at times, shoves. Like his sounds, Smokie's body contact and movement held a vast array of meanings. Indeed, Smokie's sounds and body movements blended with mine to produce not only meaning but also feeling. There's no question, for me, that Smokie and I lived on a plane that brought the non-human animal and human animal together in a way which is not only distinct from, but also defies, any conventional human understanding of nature and of the non-human animal, and their relation to any usual understanding of the human and of the social.

Smokie has taught me a great deal about non-human animal life and about human life. He has taught me a great deal, too, of the form and shape these lives should take as they come together and how they should be lived together-to-gether. He has also taught me a great deal of what it means to be blind and of the feel of blindness. Most crucially, Smokie showed me a blindness that I hadn't even imagined and, I am certain, a blindness that surpasses any conventional human understanding of what it means to be blind and, ironically, of what it means to see. Smokie continues to teach me these lessons and, like his teaching and my learning, our friendship and love grow and continue to do so.

These letters are influenced by the work Dan and I have done and continue to do as we draw upon various fields of inquiry such as cultural studies, Black, queer and gender studies, Indigenous studies, animal studies, and, of course, disability studies. These fields, while different from one another, bear the similarity of their exploration of marginality. In this sense, all of these fields have much to teach us about blindness and human/non-human animal relations, and much to teach us as well of where different expressions of marginality belong, both in the world and together. These fields of inquiry have greatly influenced how I do my work in disability studies. Perhaps most importantly, they have shaped the ways I have come to understand blindness as a cultural phenomenon more than a biological one. This understanding, in turn, has shaped the way I experience my own blindness and how I live with it and in it. Of course, this influence does not come without its shortfalls. Indeed, these shortfalls provoke some of what Smokie says in his letters to Dan. These provocations may serve as a foundation for the further development of the field of disability studies and may even provoke the cultivation of a field we might call blind studies.

Smokie occasionally makes reference in his letters to Dan to some of the writings in these fields of inquiry. As a way to indicate where Smokie gleaned his references, I write endnotes in my voice. In these notes, I attempt to explain how Smokie could have heard of the works to which he makes reference. The following letters are also framed with the friendship that Dan and I share. In them are myriad references to this friend-ship and to what Smokie would have made and makes of it. And to the Beatles. Dan and I are Beatles fanatics. They are integral to our friendship. He and I argue, albeit affectionately, about who was the greatest Beatle. Dan says Paul and I say John. In these letters, Smokie contributes to the continuing dialogue Dan and I have on the Beatles and contributes, too, to the Paul/John debate. Who you think the greatest Beatle is, is a choice I leave to you. But, trust me, it's John.

What follows is a culmination of so much: of friendship, of life influences, of blindness, of sight, and, most especially, of love. In a sense, these letters might be read as love letters, as depictions of the love that exists between Smokie and me and how this love influences each and every friendship I have.

Toronto
August 2022

Dan Goodley

In the first of the letters that I received from Smokie, dated 13 September 2020, he congratulated me on the publication of my new book. I was delighted and surprised. It's not every day, after all, that you receive an email from a dog, especially a guide dog.

Now, I've heard and read stories about Smokie shared by other people and by one person in particular: my dear, dear friend Rod Michalko. Smokie was—and remains—a regular subject of Rod's tales. Smokie emerged in these accounts as a rather marvellous character—indeed, so marvellous that to simply refer to him as a "guide dog" feels a little demeaning. Guide dog. The words do not really do justice to the elaborate and loving stories Rod has shared. Smokie was charismatic and disruptive. He was fearless but caring. While some might say he is gone he is still very much around. And he and Rod got into various scrapes and entanglements that have made me laugh aloud and shed a tear (or seven).

But I'm getting ahead of myself now.

Perhaps already you *get* why I was so delighted and surprised to receive Smokie's email message?

There I was, one rainy autumn morning in West Yorkshire, Brexit Britain, sitting in front of my computer and surveying this most unlikely of emails. My early morning inbox tends to be filled with spam and sales messages. Damn those algorithms. But there, amid the junk, was his short, sweet, and funny message.

An email. From a dog.

So, I quickly typed my reply—trying not to overthink things—keeping with the playful vibe of Smokie's message.

I wanted to let him know that, while I felt I knew him, I really wished I'd met him in the flesh. So I tried to convey this in a brief response. I clicked the send button and wondered what might happen next.

This was the start of a correspondence that lasted for many months.

And what a time to write to one another. As the pandemic raged around us it inevitably found its way into our conversations. Fear, anger, and frustration laced our correspondence. But there was also love, contentment, Black Lives Matter, and the Beatles. They all found their place too. While the pandemic framed the discussions, it did not dictate. It turns out that we had much to ponder. Smokie's letters sustained me through lockdown. During my more grandiose moments I considered our exchanges—these fascinating conversations between a human and a dog—to be rather zeitgeisty. COVID-19 has revealed many things about the human condition, not least the inseparability of humans from their environments and "non-human life." I recall wandering through the woods near my house, one cold morning in December 2020, reflecting on the BBC news I'd googled that morning. Chinese bats were cited as an origin story of the pandemic on the very same day that Denmark culled thousands of mink afflicted with a SARS-CoV-2 variant. This was clearly not a good time to be human or animal. And yet, Smokie's letters pushed me beyond these simple categories and very real animal/human tragedies to find a more generative, hopeful place.

I came to learn through him much about the intimacy, sophistication, and care associated with his work as a guide dog. I was pushed to reconsider the very idea of "work" and to think more carefully about his guidance, alliance, and support. One recurring theme of our correspondence was our shared love of one particular human being, Rod Michalko.

Rod was rarely far from our thoughts and often central to them. Smokie and Rod had lived a tremendous life together (they had the stories to prove it), one that frames the love and friendship that Rod and I started to build over a decade ago. Sure, the pandemic has screwed up times to be "together-to-gether," but regular online catch-ups maintained our human contact. That said, the online is no replacement for the offline. Rod and I are not alone in having our relationship negatively impacted by the pandemic. Some poor souls have lost their loved ones. Others have suffered far more than we have. I want to say thank God for Smokie, as he came to vitalize an aspect of my friendship with Rod when it was most needed. Smokie also invited me to embrace some novel ways of communicating. Rod and I, like most friends, I imagine, have cultivated our relationship in various contexts. Pubs, restaurants, camping fields, cars, trains, kitchens, parking lots, and hotel lobbies are just some of the places in which we have gotten to know one another. Our relationship has also grown in academic contexts such as the seminar, lecture, written text, and conference. Who knew one could find love in academia! I have always been proud of our aptitude to move effortlessly between the formal register of the wanky academic conference and the more sweary and down-to-earth atmosphere of the dive bar. Smokie has also occupied these diverse contexts in his time with Rod. So, it came as no surprise to discover that he could speak with aplomb across various places and spaces as he pondered and questioned life.

An important space in which Rod, Smokie, and I have come to know one another is one defined by disability. All three of us have written about disability. Each of us has our own distinct personal experiences of and relationship with disability. I grew up around disability. And, later on, I was to find myself writing and researching disability. I don't want to say much more about this, only to note that disability makes a regular appearance in our letters for reasons that will become fairly apparent. Blindness and sightedness also figure prominently. And the reasons for their presence will also become quite clear (if that's not too sighted a term). Typically, academics have a tendency to seek out a quick definition of the phenomena that we find ourselves writing about. But I'm going to hold off from doing this. Inspired by Smokie and Rod, I propose that we *sit* with the phenomena of disability, blindness, and sight. Many of the questions and reflections that pepper our correspondence are informed by our engagements with literature and theory. It is possible to trace many of the ideas that we implicitly and explicitly draw upon to our reading of Animal, Black, Queer, Indigenous, and Disability Studies. Like Rod, I have added notes throughout the text: to acknowledge the inspiration of others and to encourage the reader to follow up on some of this work. It is important to recognize that these different kinds of studies—these expansive and challenging fields of inquiry—are not simply forms of scholarship that keep academics in jobs. At their most useful and provocative, these interdisciplinary fields call out inequality and cultivate forms of resistance. Disability studies, for example, is a field that Rod and I have been associated with for many years. I identify as a non-disabled person who has experienced disability throughout my family life.

My book—*Disability and Other Human Questions*—which prompted Smokie's lovely email, was my attempt to reflect upon disability and its place in my life. My own grandparents' experiences with hearing and speech impairment had a profound influence on how I have come to understand disability. As I write those words "hearing and speech impairment," I feel a sense of disconnection as I reduce my own father's parents—Horace and Dorothy Goodley—to categories. They were (and remain) complex souls that profoundly impacted the ways in which I understand normalcy, difference, and disability. Horace and Dorothy were my entry points into my relationship with disability, and disability studies was a field of inquiry that welcomed my entry. During the time period *Letters with Smokie* was written, I became ever more convinced by a simple maxim of disability studies: disability can be a *driving subject* of inquiry rather than simply an object of study. A similar statement can be made about blindness.

This book, then, is very much in the tradition of disability studies, especially in the ways in which disability and blindness are centralized as the phenomena through which to ask many human and non-human questions. And Smokie emerges as a central figure: an inevitably anthropomorphized character who, nonetheless, troubles some of the easy distinctions that we carry around with us between human/animal, nature/culture, and ability/disability. I feel that Smokie reveals himself as a theoretical provocateur. Just like Horace and Dorothy, he demands that we attend to the complexities of life rather than seeking out easy answers. But he also *guides* us through problems and possibilities, and in this sense he is very much a welcome new voice in disability studies.

Our correspondence reveals some key contributions of disability studies. One of these is the paradigm shift that disability studies agitates for: the move from the easy stories of medicalization and psychologization (sometimes referred to in the literature as medical or individual models) to the more complex narratives of disability that are created in the relational—the social, the cultural, and the political. This shift moves disability onto a plane of analysis that sits alongside other transformative perspectives such as Animal, Black, Queer, and Indigenous Studies. Politicizing disability—and blindness—is something that often feels like a new venture, even in the social sciences, arts, and humanities. Because disability is a phenomenon typically forged in the biomedical or psychological industries, its political nature is often overlooked by scholars and theorists who describe their own work as political.

Disability studies seeks to remind us all that disability says as much about society as it does about our bodies and minds. But in thinking with disability and blindness as our driving subjects of inquiry—in the company of Smokie—we are also asked to consider *more-than-human relations.* The subtitle of our book is testimony to Smokie's presence and the impact of a global pandemic. COVID-19's "zoonotic status" (a term I only learned of as a consequence of the pandemic) demonstrated beyond any doubt the global and local ways in which health and disease are reproduced at the complex interface of "human-animal ecosystems," a state of affairs that has been described as "One Health" by the World Health Organization.[2] And so, while Smokie pushed me to rethink some of the clunky ways in which I categorized humans and animals, our correspondence must be understood in the context of lockdown.

Both Smokie and the pandemic encouraged me to "exercise humility, caution, and respect for non/humans" as we contemplate the human condition.[3]

Ultimately, this is a book about love, friendship, and intimacy. It might also be a text about humans and animals. But, as I write these words, I find myself unconvinced by this simple distinction. There is clearly far more to be found in the relationships between humans and animals. This text grapples with questions of disability and the more-than-human—though it's interesting to note how rapidly these questions merge into stories. I want to acknowledge my love for Smokie and Rod, for the opportunities they've given me to sit, wander, disturb, and disrupt together-together.

Now, back to those spam messages; I need some new trainers/sneakers.

Meltham, West Yorkshire, England
August 2022

Letters *with* Smokie

Congrats!

What a beautiful one-minute advert for your new book! BTW, you look great in the video. I particularly like the blue and gold scarf draped, in a cavalier way, over your shoulders bringing out the beautiful royal blue in your shirt and aquamarine of your eyes. Lovely! Did you get new glasses? Smashing!

We've ordered your book.[1] Thanks for the shout-out to Smokie and me, beautiful Dan. However, I must speak for Smokie. If he were alive, he would speak for himself of course, but . . . His question and don't let it offend you, Smokie—he's just like that when he uses human language—he says,

> "WTF! Other Human Questions? What? Are
> you humans the only ones who can ask questions?
> So, what am I? Chopped liver? Don't answer that.
> I get it; you're just interested in the human. Start
> broadening your thinking regarding the human.
> I, and others like me, have questions too! Namely,
> who the fuck do you think you are talking about us
> while ignoring our questions? BTW, thanks for the
> mention. Between you and me, Dan, I was getting
> quite sick of dragging Rod around. Forward,
> Smokie. Right. Left. Not only that, the dude had
> no idea where he was going. If it wasn't for me—
> nothing. Nada. He would have been zero. I made

him, Dan. Anyway, enough about me. How are you? If that's not too human of a question."

Sorry, Dan. When the Smoke-ster got going on a rant, it was impossible to stop him. Take his words with a grain of salt, and he hasn't even finished reading your book; he's only on chapter four.

Brilliant book!

xxx
Rod

To Smokie; well, Rod, please can you pass this on to him.
Dear Smokie,

It's one of my main regrets in life that I never got to meet you in the flesh. The thing is, though, *that* human being that you hung around with (you know, the Canadian athlete, the one who took you in all those bars, the hard man "American Football" player, I think he goes by the name of Rod Michalko), well, he talks about you all the time. And I mean *all the time.* You, Smokie, are very much part of the stories we tell one another—Rod, Tanya, Rebecca, Ruby, Rosa, me, and many others—and while they might be human stories, they are also full of non-human stories too.

So, I suppose one way of thinking about things would be to say that while we start off with questions of the human, they soon morph, change, and bend into questions about the more-than-human. Truth is, Smokie, I think I already know you because of the tales that Rod and Tanya share about you. And I know it's not as good as meeting in the flesh (believe me, I am one handsome chap like your good self, and I know we would get on); the stories that are told about you do mean you are very much part and parcel of our world (the human and non-human).

Thanks as always for the provocation. And thank you, sincerely, for being around to permit Rod to come up with that really funny gag about you being a "blind dog."[2]

Much love,
Dan

Hi Dan,

I really have to say I wasn't expecting you to write back to me, not directly anyway. Every other time someone wanted to say something to me, they told Rod and then he told me. You were the first one that got back to me, right to me. I have to say, I like this better—talking direct like this.

The other thing that happened for the first time was when I told Rod what I thought about your book, he said he would pass it on to you directly from me, word for word. I didn't think much of it at the time. The truth is, I never thought I could speak to anyone directly except Rod, and I didn't think anyone else could speak right to me except Rod. That's why I'm so surprised to hear from you.

This place, this other world, as you humans like to call it, is pretty cool. Got the rest of them with me a few years back, all three of them, so it's even better.[3] It's very peaceful and you never get tired no matter how much you run and play. You never get hungry either, no matter how much you eat. Lots of trees, grass, places to swim—love it. Just love it. Sure miss Rod, though—Tanya too. But, I talk to the guy every day. He fills me in on what's going on, keeps me in the loop. They're back in Toronto now; always thought they'd get back there one day. But, I guess without us . . .

Anyway, enough about that.

You guys met, I mean you, Rod, and Tanya, you met a long time ago, around 2009, wasn't it? Wasn't it someplace in

Arizona at one of those conferences they used to go to about disability studies? I was gone for a few years by then, I mean, to that other world place. I sure was touched when Rod told me you read the book he wrote about us. That meant a lot to me—how much you and Rebecca enjoyed that story—it really did. So, you met way back and, as you humans like to say, the rest is history—all disability studies and all friendship. I sure have been enjoying all the stories about this friendship you guys have. I always let Rod know about what I think of the stuff he's been doing and writing, stuff about this disability studies thing too. But, this is the first time, like I said, that someone other than Rod got back to me directly about disability, so let me tell you more about what I think about what you said.

Like I already told you, I reacted mostly to the title of your book. Rod told me about your book, about some of the chapters and how you were writing about your relationship to disability and all of that. He hasn't read it all the way through yet, so we haven't discussed it fully. I'm sure we will as soon as he reads it and I'm sure that Tanya will have something to say about it too.

The thing about your title—*Disability and Other Human Questions*—is the last part, the other human questions part. I get it; there is the question of disability and then there's other human questions. I'm thinking this means that disability is a human question and that's what I wrote you about before. My point was that I don't think disability is strictly a human question and, I don't know what other human questions you had in mind, but sticking strictly to the human is where you humans make a mistake.

I guided Rod for nearly ten years and, when I say I guided him, I mean everywhere—all around Toronto and then later all around Antigonish, Nova Scotia. We took subways, street-cars, buses together, travelled on trains, planes, and even boats. We did everything together. This sounds like a lot of work to humans. In fact, you humans call us working animals, or even worse, service animals; I hate that name. I loved hanging with Rod, taking him to all the places he wanted to go and even to some places he didn't. I remember one time in Antigonish, compared to Toronto, it's really small. They had a summer fair, tiny little midway, food stalls, and the thing I loved best, a barn with all kinds of animals: cows, sheep, horses, you name it, they had it. I love animals, Dan. We went into that barn and the first thing I saw was this big cow. It was in the stall, of course, with a gate. But, there were spaces between the boards of the gate and that cow and we stood there, nose to nose, for a long time getting to know each other. Then, Rod got me going. I didn't want to, so I took my time. But he always thought he was in charge, so eventually, I let him think that and we moved out of the barn, but I went real slow so I could check out all the other animals. When we got out, Rod gave me one of those vague commands he sometimes did when he wasn't sure. No way he could have known how to get around the fairground—when to tell me left, right. So, he did what he always did in situations like this, he let me be in charge. Quite honestly, he had no choice. So, what I did is guide him around the fairground, slowing down a little at places where I thought he might get a kick out of the sound, but I kept my eye on that barn. I kept guiding Rod around and around the fairground until I knew he was pretty much lost and then . . . I took him right back to the barn. Rod was great about it. He just laughed, scratched me behind my ears, and told me I was a good boy, and then

I laughed and we hung around the barn for a while. Rod was good that way. I guided him where he needed to be and he let me do what I needed to do. Not all of my guide dog friends have blind guys like Rod, that's for sure.

My point is, Dan, I hung around with a blind guy for most of my life, and blindness, I bet you, like all disabilities, is way more than a human question. That's why I like what you wrote to me. You said something like while you start off with questions of the human, they soon morph, change, and bend into questions about the more-than-human. Now, this is good stuff. The thing is, I spent my entire life with humans. I was trained to be a guide dog. In the dog world, we call this postgraduate education. Cool, eh. The only thing I'm not sure of is that this difference between human and non-human fits my experience, not exactly. I get how human stories can morph into non-human, but do you think it goes the other way around, too? Sometimes I think human questions, non-human questions, human stories, non-human stories, what's the difference? There has to be one, I guess, but what is it?

Those are just a few thoughts I was having about what you wrote me, Dan. Rod tells me all about you, Rebecca, Ruby, and Rosa and how you guys are like family. I wish I had met you in the flesh, too, but I really feel I know you from the tales Rod tells about you and, believe me, there's lots of them. I know you're right, Dan, we would definitely get on and, you're also right, we are two handsome chaps. By the way, that blind dog thing—that wasn't a gag—someone actually said that about me. Fucking humans.

Much love,
Smokie

Dear Smokie,

Fucking humans! Ha! I can tell where Rod gets his sense of humour from.

I am delighted you replied. Soooooo delighted. I was touched by you getting back to me. I have to be honest that I found myself getting rather emotional when I first wrote to you. And, when I got your reply, well, you got me again. Let's say a tear was shed. I had a moment (as they say). I am disappointed we never met in the flesh but I feel in some small way that our conversation is a way of connecting and this makes me chuffed. Do they say "chuffed" in Canada? If you're "chuffed" in Northern England then you are "happy" and "content." You have to say it with a Northern drawl.

There's so much to write to you about. Where do we start? I feel we have so much time to make up! I also wonder of course what Rod has told you about me, Rebecca, and our girls, Ruby and Rosa. That first meeting in Arizona was a blast. I finally got to meet Rod and Tanya at a disability studies conference held in Tucson in 2009. I was a big fanboy of Rod's and Tanya's disability studies writing. They always say "never meet your heroes" but I'm so glad that I met Rod and Tanya. What struck me about them both is how much fun they were/are and also how they're big on community. Perhaps we can come back to this word (and others) in our letters at some point later ("community" I mean, not "big"). But, for now, what really struck me about them in their doing of community was two things. First, they appeared to have supported and brought along a group of doctoral researchers (all doing disability studies, by the way) to accompany them to the conference. I sat by the pool of the conference venue earlier in the day and was a little envious of this big group of young, cool-and-happening hipster disability studies dudes and dudettes drinking and laughing by the swimming pool enjoying the sun. I never did that during my PhD! It was only later that I learned they were with R and T.

Second, after making the point of introducing myself to Rod and Tanya, I was invited back to the balcony of their room. They had refilled the mini-bar with a mountain of beer and wine and were hosting what can only be described as an after-show party! I never met academics like that before; British academics can be a little staid. The idea of hanging out with them was very seductive. The other thing I should say, Smokie, is that meeting them could not have come at a better time. I'd just found out that Rebecca's mum was not very well. So, you can imagine, I'd flown to the U.S., landed, got into my hotel and then rang home only to hear that Rebecca was really upset and worried about her mother. I'd then spent the rest of the day ringing around to organize an early flight home. And I did fly back—the day after I met Rod and Tanya. So, our meeting was a flash in the pan, but much needed. They were really supportive. They listened. They reached out. And they supplied the beers; what more do you need, eh? Why am I telling you this? Well, I suppose I'm trying to find out what Rod told you about our meeting but also to give you a little context in terms of how you are spoken about, Smokie.

You see, what Rod does when he talks about you is that he always gives context. By this I mean that the stories I hear of you guiding him through the world are always stories of places, of people, of humans, and non-humans. They are stories of physical spaces, of relationships, of negotiations, of movement. These are tales of specific times in history (because after all Rod is one old man). And of different geographies. And they are intimate too. I am struggling to think of a story of you and Rod which is not greeted with laughter or an "ahhhhhh." This leads me back to some of the questions you posed in your last letter. You wrote: "The only thing I'm not sure of is that this difference between human and non-human fits my experience, not exactly. I get how human stories can morph into non-human, but do you think it goes the other way around, too? Sometimes I think human questions, non-human questions, human stories, non-human stories, what's the difference? There has to be one, I guess, but what is it?" Jesus, Smokie, you can tell you had a postgraduate education. These are really difficult questions. I'm going to be a typical academic here and dodge the questions (at least for now). I'd like more context. I'd like to know some more about where you're coming from. You wrote that you spent a lot of time in the human world: but can you give me a bit more detail? How the hell did you end up guiding a human in the first place? And, to be a bit more personal here, are you happy with me referring to you as a non-human?

I just want to mention one other observation. I find Rod most animated in the world when he is talking about either (1) John Lennon, (2) Tanya, or (3) you. Not sure how you feel about this. And by the way, I'm sure you'll agree that Paul was and is the true Beatles legend.

Cannot wait to hear back from you Smokie.

Much love,
Dan x

Hi Dan,

You wrote back again and—to me! Rod said you would. But you know what he's like; sometimes he says things that are kinda true, but not, not that he's making up shit, even though he does that a lot. But I thought he was just trying to make me feel good and encourage me. He did that a lot back in the day, and he's damned good at it. I was emotional and I had a tear in my eye when I got your letter.

"Chuffed." Never heard that word here in Canada, except from Rod. Since he and Tanya have been travelling over to the UK to see you and Rebecca, Ruby, and Rosa, he's been speaking all kinds of Brit words. He says, "I'll ring you" instead of "I'll call you." He says "it's meant to be warm today" instead of "it's supposed to be warm today." He says "pavement" instead of "sidewalk." He even says "well done" instead of "good job." You know what I think? I think Rod's become an anglophile, that's what I think. I would have had to learn a new language if he and I ever went to the UK. I could have done it, Dan. First place I lived with Rod and Tanya, Jessie, and Sugar was in an Italian neighbourhood of Toronto. After about a month or so, people in the markets, in the bank, and even in Rod's favourite bar started speaking to me in Italian. They would say "aspetti" instead of "wait." So, I think I could have picked up Rod's way of speaking Brit.

You asked how I got into this guiding thing. By the way, you don't actually call me non-human like you said. You say non-human in the same way I say you are human. But, you call me Smokie like I call you Dan. So, that's good; but, we'll have to get back to the non-human/human thing later, I think. Anyway, it's not clear to me, this guiding thing, I mean. I don't really remember a time when I wasn't learning human words, and my first memories were of words like sit, stay, down, come, good boy—words like that, not whole sentences. You have to remember, too, that my first memories came when I was only about two or three months old (for a human, that's already getting up there). I remember the people I was living with were a great couple. They had a pool which I loved and a couple of kids. I think that's why I always loved swimming so much, even though some humans tell me that because I'm a Labrador retriever swimming is an instinct. It sure wasn't for little Cassis, Tanya's Lab. Whenever humans talk about us—non-humans—they say "it's instinct," but, when they talk about themselves, they never say that; the closest they get is "genetics" or "hard-wired," which I think means the same thing. I also think living with that family is where I learned to love kids—no instinct there, just love. I loved kids right up until the end. Next time you see Rod, ask him to tell you a few stories about me and kids.

The first actual guide dog thing I remember was that the people I was living with used to put a little jacket-like thing over my back with a sign that said "guide dog in training." Just to be clear, at the time I didn't know it was a guide dog thing. I knew that only later; looking back at it, I think you call that hindsight or something. Anyway, when they put that little jacket on, I got quite excited because every time they did we went somewhere cool like the mall, on streetcars, even subways. They took me wherever there was a bunch of people, even into restaurants. They were kinda strict, though. I couldn't stop and sniff anything, couldn't go up to little kids and lick their faces, couldn't try to get food at the restaurants, couldn't do any of that stuff—just had to walk, nice and calm, and I had to pay a lot of attention because sometimes my people would do strange things. I remember, one time they started to cross the street and there were still cars coming. I didn't want to disobey them, I mean, that's what we do, obey humans. But, fuck! They were gonna get killed and they were gonna kill me! So, I wouldn't go. They said "good boy" about a million times, gave me a bunch of treats, so I learned pretty quickly I should pay attention. Quite honestly, I really loved paying attention. Hanging out in the human world— absolutely fascinating. Maybe we'll have to talk about this sometime later, Dan; maybe we'll talk about what's fascinating for me about the human world and what's fascinating for you. I'll tell you some of the stuff Rod and I used to say on this topic and still do.

This guy, Greg was his name, used to come to where I lived with my people every month or so. Nice guy; he'd put on my little guide dog jacket and take me for a walk. We'd go everywhere—busy streets, supermarkets, schools (I loved that, especially all those little kids), even buses and streetcars. He'd really put me through the paces—sit, stand, down, stay, all that stuff. He even taught me left, right, and forward. It was a lot of fun.

The next thing that happened was nothing short of heart-breaking. Greg shows up to my home one day. He puts my little jacket on like usual, but this time we get into a van. We don't go for a walk. So far so good; something new; I love doing new things. Next thing I know, we're at the guide dog school. I made the cut. I was now going to start training to be a guide dog. What I didn't know is that I would never be going home again. I can't believe how you humans build heartbreak right into how you construct this world of yours.

The first month or so was devastating. I really missed my people. But then, I got real close to Greg. He was the one who was training me to be a guide dog. The training was pretty tough, but I loved it. Figuring out how to get around all the obstacles they stuck in the way was really a lot of fun. I met a bunch of other dogs, too. All of us were training to be guide dogs.

Greg was training about four or five of us, a string of dogs—that's what he called it. We trained every morning and afternoon. Greg took us out of the kennel and we went to either downtown Oakville (which is where the school was) or we went in the van and trained in downtown Toronto (which was about an hour drive from Oakville). I loved all this training, especially in Toronto; it was nice and busy, lots to figure out.

Then, I noticed after four or five months or so, blind people would come around and each of us on Greg's string would be matched up with one of them. They stayed at the school and we'd hang out with them the entire month. Training with them and living with them in their room. After a month of training, all the other dogs went home with their blind people. I didn't! Greg said I was too fast. Can you believe it? Too fast! I thought that was a good thing. I used to zip those blind people around Oakville and Toronto while we were training, thinking it was fun. Too fast; turned out it was too fast. More heartbreak.

I was really getting down and I was getting bored, too. I was at that school a little over six months and not one blind person wanted me. I was so down I couldn't even get pumped up when Greg took me out of the kennel for training or when he would take me to his home on the weekend sometimes. I had no idea what was gonna happen.

This is when Rod showed up. He came along one day with a fresh batch of blind people. They paired me up with him. At first, I was still down. I was glad to be with him in his room, but I knew after a month he'd be gone. So, I tried not to get too close to him. That was hard.

Then, something surprising happened. Rod and I were working around Oakville with Greg and the rest of the dogs and their blind people one day and Rod gives me the command "hup hup." That's guide dog talk for "speed up; let's rock." I'm thinking—"all right!" He did the same thing when we trained in Toronto; walking down Yonge Street, real busy, he says, "Smokie—hup hup." I kicked it into another gear and we rocked. Things were looking up. I found out only later that Rod was my last chance. If we didn't work out, I would have gone back to my family, you know, just a pet, well trained, but just a pet.

Here's another great thing that happened; I met Tanya, his partner. She used to come to Oakville every few days to visit Rod; I loved those times and I always felt really bad when she left. But, so did Rod, so we were sad together.

After a month, Tanya shows up and the three of us—Rod, Tanya, and I—head to Toronto—my new home. That's the scoop on how I became a guide dog, Dan. Sorry about the long story, but once I get started talking about stuff, I just keep going. Rod and I are the same this way—don't you think?

You asked me what Rod told me about you, Rebecca, and the two girls, Ruby and Rosa. Remember how you said that he talks all the time about me? Same with you, Rebecca, and the girls. After he met you in Arizona, that's all he could talk about. Dan this, Dan that, Dan said this, Dan said that. And, it was the same when Rod and Tanya got back from their first trip to the UK, except instead of Dan this and Dan that it was all of you. "Rebecca has the greatest voice ever in the history of humankind. Ruby and Rosa are the two smartest, funniest, and best-looking girls"—they were only eight and nine years old at the time—"in the entire world." And it didn't stop; it kept going over the years and still hasn't stopped. Our home in Toronto (which, by the way, I'm still with them) has more stories about the four of you than it does furniture. I really feel I know you, Dan, and that I know Rebecca, Ruby, and Rosa too. To this day, I wish I had been with Rod in the flesh back in 2009 when he started to meet his UK family.

I wasn't exactly sure what you meant when you said Rod always gave a context when he spoke of me. Incidentally, I'm glad to hear that Rod speaks of me in a way that makes people laugh or feel good. He can be a great storyteller . . . when he wants to be. When he talks about you and the three Rs, as he calls them, it's always stories. Everything he says about all of you is said in stories. Is that what you mean by context? To be quite honest, Dan, I can't imagine anyone saying anything without context; I can't imagine anyone speaking with no context. Can you? I wonder if when people say things, they sometimes, or maybe even often, don't know they're speaking in a context. Maybe when they speak they don't realize they're telling a story. Rod always said that it was up to us (wasn't ever sure who "us" was), but he always said it was up to us to listen to the story and to hear it when people speak. I think the old guy had something there.

By the way, we should talk about this word "community" sometime and maybe even talk about the word "big" too—lots to say about that. I hear that word, I mean "community," all the time around here. Those academic friends that Rod and Tanya have—they use it constantly. Sometimes they hook it up with another word they always use "folks." They never say people anymore, just folks. They say "community folks." And, you know what they mean by that? Anybody who isn't part of the university—community folks—they're community folks. Strange AF.

The questions about the human and non-human differences and the differences between the human world and the non-human world you threw back to me are a lot more than interesting, as you suggest. They're also a lot more than difficult questions. Here's the funny thing, Dan—I think there are questions that should not be answered. Get it? Questions that shouldn't be answered. Let me tell you what I mean, at least let me give it a shot. Instead of looking for answers to these questions, maybe we have to look for the answers that generated these questions. All right, Dan, that's not a question, so you can't dodge it. I'll tell you another thing: this difference between the human and the non-human, the human world and the non-human world—well, those are differences that you humans make. Like I said, the question isn't about the differences themselves, it's about how these differences came about. How is it possible to ask questions about these differences and what these differences are? Maybe the differences between the human and the non-human and between the human world and the non-human world are not differences at all. Maybe they're distinctions.

I'll leave you with that, Dan. Another thing—Rod described the cover of your new book, the one about disability and other "human" questions. To be honest, I am pretty sure Tanya described it to him and then he described it to me. It's all full of wheelchairs! All right, one is upside down and, as Rod says, in Brit, that's controversial. But, disability—wheelchair—the same? You could have had a picture of me on the cover all decked out in my harness. Rod still has it, by the way, my harness, I mean. Oh—the question of who is the true Beatles legend—which, by the way, is a real question—the answer, without question, is John. Remember, Dan, I'm in a place where I heard the answer from the legend . . . himself.

Coming at you with love,
Smokie

16TH NOVEMBER 2020

Dear Smokie,

What a pleasure. Your letter from Rod's email dropped in my inbox on Sunday morning. "Dropped" is such a 2020 word. "That new song has dropped." "Have you seen the new season of *The Crown* has dropped on Netflix?" "I'll drop the document with you by Wednesday afternoon." Dropped. I think I like this word. It seems to me that when something "drops" it has arrived in the world; ready to be discovered, devoured, binge-watched, or listened to. I have that feeling with your letters. Rod drops them. I quickly open and read them. I then let your thoughts, questions, and provocations percolate for a day or two. I don't want to offer a glib or overexcited reply. We have so much time to make up. So, I want to cherish our moments of conversation. I want to give you some considered offerings back by way of a letter. But, I don't want to overthink things either. I don't want to get all academic on you here. By that, I mean, I don't want to pull our correspondence immediately into my day job of academia, where I seem to spend some of my time ripping apart some of the most intimate stories by way of theoretical analysis. I'm not saying that *all* analysis is unhelpful, that *all* academia is dull, or that *all* academics are boring. But you name me one person who would happily be locked in a room with an academic for an hour or three. I want to learn some more about your life and loves, Smokie. And I want to know where you're coming from, not least in relation to the whole human/non-human thing. And I want to sit with your thoughts for a time before coming back to you. Sitting with something is an interesting one. I remember Tanya hosting an event in Toronto sometime back where she encouraged us all to "sit with ideas." I know that the word "sit" is familiar to you. And I'm not being facetious here. And I wonder how we might be sitting together as we write to one another.

You're right about context, of course. Good stories say as much about the teller as they do about the world around the teller. Stories are context. And you are a wonderful storyteller, Smokie—not least because you're funny—and it seems to me you have loads to say about human and non-human worlds (again, we'll come back to this). So, when I said that Rod gives context, I think what I should have said is that when Rod tells stories of you, him, and Tanya, he is always filling in the details, moving toward the punchlines but always carefully ensuring that we come to know you. I don't think a "Smokie story" is ever offered cheaply.

I know these stories are cherished. There is joy and sadness to these tales. You're missed. But you're also ever-present. In appealing to the word "context" I was wanting to open up some more about how you and I got here: to this moment, to be having this correspondence and sharing these thoughts. I worry a little that I might be relying too much already on what I think I know about you when I'd like to learn more. And, equally, I'd like to give a little more context—some more stories—that give away a bit more about why I ended up meeting Tanya and Rod in the first place (and why you and I are now in touch with one another). I don't want to assume that you and I already know these stories. So let me add to my earlier account about meeting Rod and Tanya. Perhaps I'm giving you a little origin story.

Disability is one reason we ended up meeting. It was the main reason. I'll admit the fact the conference was in sunny Arizona was a big pull. And the hotel having a pool closed the deal. But the reason I flew to this stateside conference—and why I knew of Rod, Tanya, and you—was because of disability. The conference was a disability studies event, bringing together researchers, writers, artists, activists, and practitioners all engaged with disability.[4] It was really exciting to be there. To put faces to names. To drink beer with humans that I'd only originally encountered in text. To be with others engaged with disability. I came to disability because of my own family experiences with disability. It was something that was part of my life. Disability was ordinary to my family in many ways. But over the years I'd learned that disability was treated as extraordinary, as a tragic deficiency or failing within people. Disability studies turned these ideas upside down: reconceptualizing disability as not only an aspect of difference and diversity (to use your words) but as an opportunity and driving subject through which to think again about the world. And you, Smokie, were part of this new way of thinking—disability studies—as a key player in Rod's work: writing which has come to be known as part of the disability studies literature. As Rod wrote about his own blindness and his relationship with you, he offered readers (like me) insights (can we use that word alongside blindness, I wonder) into some very intimate moments that you two shared. I loved his book *The Two in One*. I didn't know you could write like that and be an academic. And I suppose that's also what I meant by context in my earlier letter: sitting with and detailing moving through the world with you. So, while I agree with you that all stories rely on context, I think some storytellers don't sit enough with the details of life. And with this in mind, I take your point about the use of the wheelchair image on the cover of my book. I know Tanya's written about this, about the dangers of limiting the feel and complexity of disability through the lazy deployment of the wheelchair symbol. What can I say? I was washing my hair when I missed the email about the book cover. Not really. I haven't washed my hair in a decade. I think I was happy to go with the publisher's design; the wheelchair image is a quick and easy way of symbolizing disability, I suppose. But I think if we stick with this simplistic representation then we're in trouble. And I think we'll discuss this more: the symbols and meaning of disability.

There's nothing simple or easy about your story, Smokie. That family sounded lovely. They had their own pool? As we say here in the North of England: "Someone's doing well." I didn't know you'd lived with kids. And I'd never really thought about the fact that you've known about human words all your life. Of course you had, and never more so than when you were learning and enacting guiding. I think I have some idea what your answer might be, but I wonder why you dislike the service dog label? As you put it, heartbreak is built into the ways in which humans negotiated your involvement with guiding. You write, "we have to look for the answers that generated these questions." If the answer is "service dog," then I'm already worried about the question! And here I think we need to talk some more about heartbreak. It seems to be important. You reminded me of an exchange between my dad and granddad many moons ago.

My dad (Alan) was a teenager at the time. Rock 'n' roll had hit Nottingham. One day he was listening to some Elvis and he asked my granddad (Horace):

"Why are there so many songs about love and heartbreak?"

"I can't think of anything better to sing about," Horace replied.

At this point, can I come back to the idea of community and your views on this? Now, this concept is a big one in our house. Not least because I live with Rebecca who is a professor of community psychology. So we have to be very careful here, Smokie . . . very careful. If we upset the better half, you're on your own, pal! When I say R and T "do community," I mean that they take joy in being with others, bringing others together, supporting one another. In contrast there are lots of people I have known who aren't really into community: they are called members of the British Conservative Party. OK, only half-joking there. I think being "into community" is about opening yourself up to connecting with others. And these interrelations include those categorized as humans and non-humans. You'll see that I'm engaging in that very human practice of distinguishing between humans and those that are not human. As you mention, this is a very human distinction—created differences between humans and non-humans, for example—but what happens when distinctions lead to discriminations? I think that humans tend to centre themselves as the main concern and, in so doing, undervalue the lives of non-humans. I'd never thought about the heartbreak of being pulled from one family to another: as you wrote in your story. I'd only considered how great it was for Rod, that you'd joined his family with Tanya and provided for Rod many shared adventures through your guiding. I'm sorry you had to go through that experience, Smokie—of being pulled from pillar to post. I once read in some academic's book that humans tend to understand non-human animals in three ways: they either love and pet them, are scared of them, or want to eat them.[5] Maybe I could add to this list: humans like to work animals. This is a gross simplification, of course, but it at least recognizes the limitation that humans have with the ways in which they understand non-human animals. In distinguishing themselves from animals, humans blow hot air up their own arses and devalue non-human animals. This might partly explain why I never acknowledged what you went through in your life pre-Rod. Am I right, though, to suggest you would have felt this pain? Are we in danger of humanizing your story through the use of very human words such as heartbreak (you know, like the instinct/hard-wired stuff you mentioned)? Or are these the kinds of questions that we really should not answer?

You're not wrong about Rod becoming an anglophile. It's sad, isn't it? It feels like he's discarding his true Winnipegger roots. I'd rather be from Winnipeg than Manchester. If it makes you feel any better, I should point out that this ruining of people's identities through language and culture is a two-way street. Last week, Rebecca and I were chatting online with our eldest daughter, Ruby. She's in Manchester studying social anthropology. And she started one of her stories with the following line—you'll love this—"remember when we spoke to the lovely server in the restaurant that day in Manchester. . . ." Server?! Server?! Before R and T came along, she'd have used words like waitress, waiter. . . . I've also noticed more and more young people in Britain adding the word "like" to the beginning, middle, and end of sentences. I blame you guys over the pond. All this, like, hanging around with Canadians is, like, messing with the vocabularies of, like, young people.

Anyway, I'll "drop" this with you now via Rod's email.

Say hi to John from me. And when you do bump into him, can you ask him: in 1969, at the height of his powers, was Ringo the best drummer in the world?

Your friend,
Dan x

Hi Dan,

A pleasure for me, too. Every time I receive a letter from you, I'm not only chuffed, as Rod would say, I'm also still thrilled that you're writing me—through Rod, of course—but still to me! We'll have to say something about this human/ non-human communication, a communication that seems mediated by a human. This is going to involve, I think, me telling you a little something of how I (a non-human) communicated the world to Rod. The world communicating to Rod (a human) with a non-human mediator (me). Maybe next letter, what do you think?

I agree, *drop* is an interesting word. I don't think it's a strictly 2020 word as much as it is a 2020 use of the word. I'm old enough to remember—don't forget, one of my years is seven of yours—the word "drop" being used differently. "Are you gonna drop by?," "She just dropped in," "Can I drop this off at your place?," "Drop by; we'll have some kibble." Stuff like that. It's got a similar flavour in 2020, but, as you say, it's a little different. It's probably more that online thing you were speaking about.

I love how you said that our letters just got dropped off to us. Well, you actually said Rod dropped my letters off to you, but it goes both ways. You just dropped right into my life when Rod told me about the title of your new book. By the way, he tells me all kinds of stuff that you're doing—books you publish, papers, conferences, places you visited (Finger

Lake! A house right on the lake! Wish I was there! I love to swim!). And he tells me about what Rebecca and the girls are getting up to (Both in university? It seems like only a little over a year ago—sorry, for you eleven or twelve years ago—that Rod first told me about them; eight and nine years old and now in university. Wow!). Like I was saying, the title of your book, that's how you dropped into my life. But, here's the funny thing: you were in it for a long time before that. Is it possible that the same thing can get dropped many times over and still be as fresh, as exciting, as new, and get discovered yet again? Is that possible?

You said you don't want to "offer a glib or overexcited reply" to my letters. You want them to "percolate for a day or two." It's the same for me! But, even after your thoughts and questions and provocations percolate with me for a day or two and then I respond, they keep percolating! What do you think? Strange.

I'm very happy and very thankful to you for not wanting to "get all academic on my arse." It's not that I haven't had any experience with that; I had more of that than I ever wanted. Don't forget, Rod and Tanya, both of them, were and still are academics, even though Rod says he's retired. What's that other 2020 word "you people" (meaning "you humans") use nowadays—denial, that's it. He's in denial thinking he's retired. I just let him think that. I used to do that back in the day when I guided him. I got him outta so many messes. When we were in areas we had never been before, he didn't have a clue. I'm the one who got us oriented and knew what the hell we were doing. He was sure proud of himself. He did say I was a good boy and thanked me for stuff, but he still thought he had something to do with it. Denial. I just let him think that; you know how humans are, being one yourself. I gotta tell you this.

This one time, Rod, Tanya, and I were shopping in an underground shopping centre located underneath the corner of Bloor and Yonge—huge place. We wandered around a little, stopped into a few stores; then, my people decided to have a coffee. So, they did. Rod took my harness off and let me lie down under the table to relax. He was good that way. The trainers in the school always tell blind people not to take the harnesses off of their dogs in public. But Rod wasn't like that. When I wasn't working—like when he was having a coffee, more often it was a beer, he'd take my harness off and let me relax, too. Then, they decided it was time to go. Rod stood up, hooked me up (that's what we called putting my harness on—hooked me up), and we were ready to rock. Thing is, they, both of them, didn't have a clue how to get out of there. Fucking humans. So, I knew it was up to me and I was ready to motor. But I did the proper guide dog thing and waited for a command. Rod likes it when he thinks he's in command. I waited for Rod to say, "Okay, Smokie baby, it's up to you. Get us outta here. Let's go out." A few minutes after he gave me what he thought was a command, I had the two of them out on Bloor Street, right where they wanted to be, right at the place we entered the damn mall. To tell you the truth, Dan, I love doing this. After a few months of being with Rod, I got a real sense, not just of what he wanted, but of what he needed. We sort of grew up together in blindness. Man! What the? I don't know what the hell that means, Dan. But I'm thinking you're gonna have something to say about that and you're gonna ask me more about it. I think I'm getting to know you a little bit too.

Getting back to what you were saying, I also cherish these letters we're writing to one another. You dropped into my life in 2009 when you first met Rod and he told me all about you. And, like I was saying earlier, you've been dropping in ever since. But these letters are different somehow. This time you're dropping in—right to me! It's like these letters are more than a drop. It's like the drop is hanging around for more than just a one drop.

Just so you know, I've spent—man, I can't even count the hours—not in just one room but many rooms with academics—not my most fave non-human-to-human activity, I'll tell you that. Rod moved in and out. I loved that about him. He could move into the academic world, act just like one of them, and then move right out again and hang with me. I really did love that. I also loved how he used to hang, and still does, with a lot of non-academic people. Got to admit, the dude was pretty good that way.

You're right, I'm very familiar with the word "sit." I learned to sit when I was really young, when I was still living with my first family. I didn't really like it at first. It seemed like sitting was part of the ritual of humans training us non-humans to obey them. Humans want us to sit when they want us to sit. They want us to stop doing whatever it is we're doing and . . . sit. Even though I didn't like it, it wasn't really a big deal. "Sit." They would tell me to sit and I sat, no biggie. They sure thought it was; they even went so far as to say what a good boy I was and gave me treats when I sat when they told me to. Sit—get a bunch of praise—and done. Piece of cake and, like I said, I got treats. Different story for those humans; they were thrilled that I learned how to sit and obey them when they told me to. At a very young age, I began learning that humans absolutely love this "giving orders" thing, being in charge. Small price to pay, though, especially, actually only, if you're with good humans.

The same kind of thing continued when they took me to the guide dog school. Sitting seemed to be a huge deal for humans, but things changed when Rod became my person. It didn't take long for "sit" to take on an entirely different meaning.

I'm not as good as are you in explaining things in human. Even when I speak to you through Rod, it's difficult for me to tell you what it is I'm thinking or feeling. So, I'm gonna give you an example. I learned this from Rod. He used to always say to his students, "Give me an example." And he does the same thing. His examples come in stories, what you academics call "narratives," I guess because you just have to academicize every word, make it sound like it's really deep. What I'm going to do, Dan, is give you an example, tell you a story, of how what I mean by "sit" took on an entirely different meaning.

One day—this was way back in Toronto—Rod hooked me up and we went out. Don't know exactly where Rod was headed. For some reason, he didn't tell me; he usually did, but on this particular day, he didn't. It didn't matter. It was a great day in late April, I remember. Sunny, not too hot, perfect conditions for booting it. So we did.

We must have gone about a mile or so toward the subway station, so I figured we were headed toward the university; that's where we usually went. We stopped at this little park just before the subway station as we usually did. I wandered around, did my thing, if you know what I mean, Rod gave me some water and we were off.

We went ten, maybe fifteen yards and, suddenly, my harness went completely loose. That never happened before! I thought—what the fuck! Rod didn't tell me to, but I came to a dead stop. No way was I gonna keep going. Rod wouldn't have any sense of where we were going because he couldn't feel the pull on the harness. There was no way, no way I was gonna take a chance on him getting hurt, no way. So, I stopped.

I heard Rod swear, too. He said, "Smokie! What's going on!" I gave him a sign that somehow he and I worked out over the couple of years we were together; I moved a little to my right and gave him a little nudge with my shoulder. That meant, "No clue, man." Then, I felt Rod's hand, both of them actually, on my harness. "It snapped, Smoke," he told me. "It just snapped."

Here's where "sit" comes in. Rod took my harness off, put it over his shoulder, held my leash—Rod tells me that in the UK you call it a lead—and said, "Smokie, around." That meant I should turn to my right 180 degrees and face the opposite direction to which we were standing now. I did. He squatted down beside me and asked me to sit. I did. I could tell we needed to think things over, think something through. There were three things we knew we had—one blind guy, one guide dog and one broken harness. Here's the context, Dan. We were about a mile from home and the way back meant we would guide each other. Rod would let me know which way he wanted to go and, if it was safe and if I liked it, I'd guide him. I'll tell you more about this kind of decision-making later. For now, you get what we had and the context in which we had it.

There was no way for me to guide Rod. He needed to feel the pull in my harness so that he could follow. I was nearly a full body length in front of him, on his left, as I guided him and he would follow every little move I made in that harness. Now—no harness. We sat there for a while, talking it over.

Rod squatted next to me, his arm around my shoulder; I sat and we contemplated— "How are we gonna get back home, Smoke?" I turned toward him and gave him a couple of big licks on the face. That was how I told him—"Don't worry, man. It's cool. I'll get you there." He said, "Thanks, Smoke. All we got is the leash, that's it. I'm gonna have it a little tighter than usual, so I can follow you. We're gonna head to the end of this block, wait for the light to turn green, cross to the streetcar stop, and take the streetcar back home. What do you think?" I gave him another couple of licks to let him know that I was cool with it. He gave me a tight squeeze, rubbed me behind the ears, and said, "It's up to you, Smoke. Love you. Let's hit it."

He stood and I felt the leash tighten my collar slightly; he said, "Forward, Smokie," and we hit it.

I knew it was up to me. No harness, nothing to tell Rod which way I was moving. Nothing. I love what you humans call "challenges." I get a kick out of how you humans find really nice and polite words to say things that aren't so nice and polite. It seems like you like to knock the peaks off of any exciting mountain you come across. Oh well . . . What I had to do that day was to get over that peak of that exciting mountain without a harness!

We did it; we got home. Rod gave me a couple of lefts and rights along the way, more for his own sake than letting me know which way to go. Without the harness, I had to think real quick. I'm usually about one of my body lengths in front of Rod when I'm guiding him. This time, I decided to stay only a half a length in front, and I also decided to stay really close to him, touching his left leg with my right side. It worked. I moved in slightly to tell him we were turning right, away slightly for left, and we did it. Crossing busy streets, taking the streetcar, and . . . home. As soon as we got in our backyard, Rod took my leash off, I jumped up, put my paws on his chest, gave him a lick, and started running around. I must've peed a million times; come to think of it, I pooped too. I got a shitload of treats that day, I'll tell you.

You said that I was "missed, but you are also ever-present." You know, Dan, I feel the same way. I really miss Rod and Tanya—I got the other three here with me, so that's okay; but I really miss hanging with Rod. We were together all the time, I mean, *all* the time. I went everywhere with him—well, we went with each other. Over time, guiding became more a mutual thing between us than just me. Now, there's something we need to talk about. What did you call it? Interdependence; that's right, interdependence. There's one of those nice polite words again. Whenever I hear one of those words, I'm sure grateful for my postgraduate education. I think we should talk about that one day, Dan. What sort of interdependence is the human, non-human relationship? Now, there's a question. Thing is, I'm pretty sure there's a whole bunch of answers to this question floating around. Aren't you?

You're right, though, Dan. Even though I miss Rod and Tanya so much, I'm right there with them. Rod and I talk every single day. I mean it: every day. Two or three times a week, actually two or three nights, I surprise him. I sneak right into his dreams and surprise him. Really, Dan, it's a surprise for me too. I even snuck into his dreams a whole bunch of times when he and Tanya were over there in the UK. I even snuck in there when he was staying at your house, in Meltham there, when they were staying with you, Rebecca, and the girls. Those times were a blast. Got to get those times back. Oh, I have to tell you . . . actually, I shouldn't have mentioned dreams. I have a secret about them. I'll see, maybe I'll tell you later.

It's true; Rod does tell a lot of stories about me and about everything. Most times, the stories are great, but then . . . You must feel this too, Dan, that boy can drag on. Can't he? Love him, though. I know what you mean about getting to know each other through the stories Rod tells of us. I guess you academics would say that how you and I know one another is contexted. Maybe, what you humans know about everything is contexted. How academic am I! I would love to get to know you better—on my terms. I think that's what we're doing with these letters. At the same time, I think that our letters are written and read in the context of the stories Rod tells us, stories of you, stories of me. Let me throw this out before leaving this context thing. What if, and I'm saying only *what if*, blindness is a context too? What if I told you, Dan, that I contexted Rod's blindness for him? I don't mean all by myself. I mean, what if my sense of blindness provided a new context for Rod's blindness? Since I'm way out on a limb anyway, let me go a few inches farther. What if Tanya and later, you, Rebecca, Ruby, and Rosa also contexted Rod's blindness? And, what if all of us—together!—contexted the fuck out of blindness and of everything else?

Interdependence?

When it comes to Rod and Tanya, you and I have almost the exact same origin story. It was disability (blindness) that brought Rod and me together. No other reason—blindness. I'm guessing if we unwrap this blindness thing—I think you humans call it unpacking—I suspect we'll find a lot more than not seeing, dependence, needing a guide, all wrapped up somewhere there. I suspect we'd find a lot of other things, too. But that's my origin story with Rod and Tanya too. Blindness. Disability. Just like yours.

Blindness was ordinary for me just as disability, being part of your family, was ordinary for you. After all, that's what I got my postgraduate education in, blindness—dragging blind people around so they wouldn't hurt themselves and they could get to where they wanted to go. It was like driving a cab. Instead of "get in," I said "hang on," tell me where you want to go and I'll get you there. Come to think of it, I should have installed one of those meters. My point is, that's what blindness was for me—a totally ordinary job.

Didn't take long after meeting Rod that this ordinary thing became totally extraordinary. When I was getting my postgraduate education in guiding blind people, things were dead serious. Everyone was serious: trainers, the people who ran the kennel, everyone. They let us—those of us getting an education—play around in a big field they had behind the school, and we did have fun in the evenings when we weren't training. But when we were training—serious! After I got home with Rod—see, Dan, I'm still calling it home—things changed. I'm not saying guiding Rod wasn't serious. What I am saying is that it became fun too! After a few days, I realized—man, this dude is having fun! He's really enjoying this! And then, I started having fun, too; I enjoyed it! The extraordinary thing was that it didn't take long before both Rod and I loved what we were doing. I know blindness has something to do with this, but to this day, I still can't quite figure it out. I wonder if these letters will help.

By the way, before I continue, you say that when you went to the conference in Arizona, disability studies turned your conception of disability upside down. You began reconceptualizing disability as not only an aspect of "difference and diversity"—and you said these were my words! My words! I'd never say "diversity," Dan. Never. First time I heard that word was from academics that Rod used to hang with. He still hangs with some academics, but he doesn't take them as seriously anymore. Thank Dog. I think you humans use diversity as some sort of a rationalization, actually as some sort of an excuse. Humans always seem to find a banal way to express the richness of humanity—diversity, superficial and literal difference. You wanna see diversity? Check out all the different and distinct breeds, as you humans put it, of us dogs. Now, that's diversity. Speaking of that, when I was doing my postgraduate education, one of the guide dog trainers, Leslie was her name, had a Lab, a yellow one she said, who was blind and deaf. Can you believe it? Here's the kicker—she called her, the dog, Helen. I never got to meet Helen, but I sure wish I had.

I find that humans usually don't "sit enough with the details of life," as you say. "Shit writers." Is that one of those fancy academic terms? It's a good one. Some of the people Rod used to hang with, and still does, are not only shit writers but shit storytellers. I swear, Dan, when I listen to these shit storytellers, that's what their stories sound like—shit. I'm sitting there, more often lying there, listening and I—can you believe it!—I have to fill in the context for them. If I don't fill in the context, I have no clue what they're talking about. I'm glad Rod gave you some context about me in that book he wrote. Ever since he met you, he's been giving me a lot of context about you, too.

You "haven't washed your hair in decades." Really? Rod didn't tell me you were bald. Now, there's some context I coulda used. The Blind-Bald Brothers. That's why you and Rod are so close—the BB Brothers. Thanks for that context, Dan.

I lived with kids the first year and a half of my life—which is ten years for you humans. I love kids. I remember one time Rod and Tanya's friends brought their baby over to our house. The kid was brand new, only six or eight weeks old. Rod was sitting on the floor and I was lying beside him on my stomach. The father was also sitting on the floor holding the baby about seven or eight feet away from us. I tried—I tried so hard, Dan—to crawl over to that baby without Rod noticing. I don't know what was in my head. Rod had his hand on the back of my head and neck rubbing my ears; of course he was going to notice me crawling slowly over to the baby. Who was I kidding? But I really wanted to be close to that baby and lick it all over. But Rod's hand moved and grabbed my collar. That was the end of that. Rod and Tanya used to take me and little Cassis to the schoolyard in the evenings to play. I loved chasing tennis balls, any kind of ball, and especially my Kong. I got to do this every single evening, even in the winter. The other thing I really liked about these playtimes is that once in a while, if we were early enough, those little kids would be there. Those were my favourite times.

Heartbreak is important, Dan. I learned this really quickly in the human world. I have a feeling the humans think that heartbreak belongs strictly to them. It doesn't. It's not only a human thing, it's a non-human thing, too. I'm with you on not wanting to think about the question that generated the answer "service dog." I think it might have something to do with humans; well, something to do with humans accepting us non-humans in their world. If we're going to be in their world, those humans want us to provide a service. I have to say, it didn't take long being with Rod, and then Tanya, for me to realize that I was no service dog. To this day, I'm not sure what I was or am; but no service dog, I'm not that. And, that's heartfelt; we, non-humans, have that, too.

Community psychology. Those are two pretty interesting concepts to put together and it seems even more interesting to understand what concept brought these two concepts together. That's what I mean about questions and answers; community psychology must be an answer to some question or maybe it's a solution to some problem. I think that academic world of yours has to put the brakes on looking for answers and solutions and turn its attention to looking for questions and problems. You're right about R and T. They always brought people together and they were always very supportive and still are. I remember when we got to Antigonish and they started teaching at St. FX. They were brand new. A couple of weeks into the fall term, their first term there, they invited the entire department to our house for a little get-together. There were only twelve department members, but still most of them brought their partners or friends or something, and the point is that they picked up right from where they stopped in Toronto—getting people together. "Being in community," you say, "is about opening yourself up to connecting with others." What a great definition. The only thing I would do is drop the word "about." Community isn't about opening yourself up to connecting with others, it *is* opening yourself up to connecting with others.

This sense of community does, as you say, include me and you. Of course, you humans never seem to harbour the requirement, the need, to be included, since you're human. It seems that by virtue of being human you are included with one proviso—that you open yourself up to connecting with others. That's all you humans have to do. We, in contrast, can open ourselves up to connecting with others till the humans come home and, unless humans include us, we're out there, on the margins, at worst neglected and abused and, at best, we're service animals providing all sorts of non-human services to the largely mythical needs created by humans for themselves. I'm just ever so thankful that there's people like Rod and Tanya in the human world and people like you, Rebecca, Ruby, and Rosa. There's others, too, but for the moment, the six of you are one amazing community. The most amazing thing is, like the six of you, I don't need to be included—I am.

In one of these letters, we're gonna have to open up some connections between the concepts of distinction and difference. Not that we haven't already done so, but we need to do more. You asked, "What happens when distinctions lead to discriminations?" Good question. I ask, How is it that distinctions lead to discriminations? I don't think humans create distinctions very often or very well when they do. Humans deal in difference more than in distinction and this leads to a very banal version of diversity, and it leads to discrimination too. As you wrote, "Humans tend to centre themselves as the main concern." This does lead to undervaluing the lives of non-humans, as you say and, when humans place themselves at the centre of all there is, they also place themselves as the quintessential definers of the non-human. All those non-humans that the centre allows in—not quite all the way, of course—make them feel self-righteous and then they compete with one another for who has the right to be more self-righteous. They do this by counting how much difference their particular centre lets in. In the case of non-humans like me, they allow us in but, as you suggest, only if we can work for them, be pets they can cuddle and boss around, act as showpieces, and still, as you say, many of us experience violence, violence against non-humans. We—dogs I'm speaking of now—are fiercely loyal and we love unconditionally. When this is not reciprocated, we don't stop loving and stop being loyal, we become heartbroken.

There, now I cheered both of us up. I get like that sometimes. So many of my non-humans experience violence and abuse and this also breaks my heart. I have to say, Dan, I was lucky. True, I was taken from my family and then I was taken from my trainer and, just as true, this was hard; I was heartbroken. But then Rod, and then Tanya, and then the richness of their lives. What I did for Rod soon became something that couldn't possibly be described as work or service. Somehow, I got into this blind thing, this blind experience. Funny thing, so did Rod. And then, and again I'm not sure how, our two experiences came together. Rod knew this too. He wrote an entire book about it. It was a great book. I was right beside him and heard every word of it he put on his Dictaphone. We actually wrote in bars, cafes, as well as at home—did I just say we? That's a new thought. I remember giving him little nudges when I thought he was writing something ridiculous. Once in a while he would say, "Okay, okay, Smokie." He once said this in a bar, I remember, and the waiter—I like to use waiter instead of server, too—asked him if everything was okay. I just laughed.

I like what you said about humans understanding animals; they love us, are scared of us, or want to eat us. This last thing gives me the creeps. You're not "in danger of human-izing my story through the use of very human words such as heartbreak." I like how you said that heartbreak is a "very human" word. Very human or not, those of us who are very non-human have feelings. We do feel. I've been in the human world for all of my life, as I said. I've learned how to hear human expressions and, through Rod, I can express these expressions, not well, but I get by. Hanging around humans, especially Rod, I've learned a lot of human expressions. They taught me a few human words at the guide dog school, but Rod and I learned a whole whack more when we got together. You know how you humans absolutely love experts? How you have experts at everything, including in us! You humans have guide dog trainers, guard dog trainers, obedience trainers—the whole nine yards (now there's a funny human expression). But here's a thought: is it possible for non-humans to be experts in humans? I know you humans have a whole whack of experts on yourselves—psychologists, physicians, educators, hairstylists (sorry, Dan), again, the whole nine yards. But check out the non-human population sometimes. Some of us become very expert in you humans.

You are one hundred percent right about language on this side of the pond. "Like"! Don't forget, Dan, I spent about ten years in university classrooms with Rod teaching all these young people. They used the word "like" so much I lost any sense of what it meant. Like, how! I had no idea what like was like. I can sure hear with better grammar than those kids can talk, I'll tell you that.

Thanks for dropping your letter on me, Dan. Let me apologize for being so wordy. Like I said, I blame Rod. Why use fifty words when five thousand will do; that was his motto. Sadly, some of it rubbed off on me. We're very, very close, so you gotta expect this. I did bump into John, the legend. I said, "John, in 1969 at the height of his powers, was Ringo the best drummer in the world?" You know what he said?—"He's not even the best drummer in the Beatles." If I woulda heard this about Ringo when John and I were still with the rest of you, I would've pissed myself! Rod did mention this to me a long time ago, but I thought he was just kidding around. But, from the legend himself! By the way, I thought it was the Beatles that brought you and Rod together, not disability studies. Thanks for letting me go on. And, thanks for getting me to think about all that stuff I experienced years ago. I got to find a way to stick to one topic per letter instead of being all over the place. Once again, my apologies. Please say hi to Rebecca and the girls for me.

xxx
Your friend—Smokie

Dear Smokie,

My god! Your letter certainly blew my mind! What have you been smoking? You can tell by the tone of writing that I am getting overly familiar with you but that's what you do with friends, isn't it? We blur the boundaries of un/acceptability and in/formality. I think we're blurring here. I wish we were smoking together too.

There's so much in your letter that got me musing about and mulling over. Of late, during my early morning walks, I've been reflecting on the many curveballs that you throw my way. Your reflections on humans and non-humans, blindness and sighted worlds, guiding and loving, joy and heartbreak, are very provocative. I love your style here, your willingness to riff. It's interesting that you've got me pondering various questions when I'm out *walking*, when we were only recently corresponding about *sitting* with ideas.

"Growing up together in blindness" is one helluva line there. You knew I'd hit upon that. What are you, some kind of mind reader? Your stories of growing up together, guiding together, and learning together in blindness really intrigue me. I was struck too with the sheer amount of walking you, Rod, and Tanya were getting yourselves involved in. Sitting and walking together in blindness. Now, by pulling out the walking theme here, I'm not advocating for walking as a special kind of thinking. I am not assuming that everyone can walk.

After all, I've got a fair number of friends in life who don't do walking. These include mates who use wheelchairs, cars, and other devices to move themselves around the world. And my daughter Ruby, well, she's never done walking. When she was about five or six years old she asked if Father Christmas could get her a wheelchair.

Like I said, walking isn't her thing.

Rosa, on the other hand. You can't stop her speeding around. So, to be a bit more inclusive, your stories seem to be about sitting and moving with blindness and sighted worlds, across human and non-human places. Moving is an interesting one, isn't it? I find myself often really moved by your writing, you know, touched by the feel of your stories. And I am struck by those moments when you stop moving—when you sit *and* settle in the world—whether that be waiting for Rod to sort his shit out with the harness or resting for a while in a coffee shop or bar, or feeling the pull of a cute baby that intrigues you. Moving and stopping. Walking and sitting. In the midst of all this toing and froing there seem to be many questions that are raised about connection, support, and love.

Your vivid accounts of moving through the world with Rod (and Tanya) are very beautiful to me because they are messing with some of the categories (or these dodgy human distinctions) that I threw at you in our earlier correspondence. The human and non-human distinction, for example, seems to lose its purchase (if it had any in the first place) in your account of moving through cafes, metros, over streets, into cars, over pavements, up steps. There is an elegance to the movement that you gave to Rod. I am struck by the pragmatism and instrumentality that the terms "guiding" and "guide dog" convey that don't capture the wonder of the movement you describe. These human distinctions don't seem to do justice to the magnificence of your journeys. You made me laugh when you discussed Rod's denial (it's not just a river in Egypt, man) and the misunderstanding that he, cough, thought he was guiding you (hilarious, such arrogance). But to be fair to the old fella, it seems to me that he was up for letting himself go, to offer himself up to the possibilities of movement with you taking the lead. And please don't excuse the pun: I think we might be onto something else here with *leads* and *leadings*.

Now, when I replied to you in my first letter, I drew on some fairly clunky distinctions between human and non-human animals. These serve us humans well. Humans set themselves up in distinction to non-humans. Here are some of the distinctions that we humans tell ourselves: Humans think and animals feel. Humans reason while animals submit to instinct. Humans occupy a higher plane associated with cognition and consciousness. Animals simply behave and respond to their urges. Humans do community. Animals hunt in packs. Humans are culture. Animals are nature. Smokie, you are challenging some of these distinctions, at least for me, through your stories. Your understandable unhappiness with the term "service dog" demonstrates not only the arrogance of humans (built into the assumption that non-human animals are there to service human beings) but also, as you say, replays some of the dangerous ways in which humans relegate, marginalize, and pathologize animals (as outside of the human imaginary). I feel bad now for even using these distinctions and raising those questions with you. Sorry. But, in a more uplifting way, your stories of being in the world with Rod seem to cut through the clunky distinctions of humans and animals. You are blurring boundaries again here, Smokie. In the context—sorry stories—that you gave me, there is a real sense of the sophisticated ways in which you and Rod negotiate the various rules, signs, norms, and systems that mark the world. I've tried to get myself around that Tube-thing in Toronto and it's not easy. Granted, I'd just had eight pints of Ontarian beer, but it was still fairly traumatic. I wonder if your success is a reflection of the sum being more than the parts: that together, you and Rod produce through your relationship the skills and capacities that pull you both through the world.

Your stories are about the possibilities, successes, and outcomes for being-in-the-world produced through your coming together. Or, to use your terms, your narratives show much is learned from "growing up together in blindness." Now, I'm not saying that blindness has to be there for human and animals to come together, but I wonder if blindness—and disability for that matter—might be as good a place as any to start to contemplate how human and non-human animals might come together in ways that challenge the arrogance of humans and the marginalization of animals. Interestingly, there have been some cool things written about disability, humans, and non-human animals—by Rod, Sunaura Taylor, and other disabled folk.[6]

I'm not trying to romanticize stuff here. We both want to stop the heartbreak, abuse, and negligence experienced by animals that are caused by humans. But I just want to throw something in here: disabled people are also subjected to heartbreak, abuse, and negligence by other human beings. There might be something that animals and disabled humans share here; it's a horrible thought but maybe one worth thinking about together. And, going back to your stories of walking (and sitting) together in the world, they show how difficult the world is to traverse and travel around (and perhaps to sit and rest within). There are barriers, inaccessible spaces, and, sometimes, unhelpful people who made life difficult for you and Rod. But you faced those tricky moments together. And that companionship at least means you are not alone, and, most importantly, you are more together. So, I wonder if "growing up together in blindness" is hinting at something you and I need to spend some time sitting and moving with: the relationships between humans and non-humans. Indeed, you mention that you'd like to tell me a little something of how you (a non-human) communicated the world to Rod. The world communicated to Rod (a human) with a non-human mediator (you, Smokie). Yes, I'd like to read more, please—I had wondered! Indeed, this might kickstart this discussion of relationships. I'm not trying to ignore other important themes of your last letter. Instead, I wonder if this idea of relationships (what has also been called mutualities, interdependencies, and interspecies relations) might be a shared interest to think about together. Might this be a way out of those clumsy distinctions: a finding of a shared space for human and non-human animal relations? And, by the way, I'm not avoiding your point about the diversity to be found among animals (as well as humans) but wonder if we might find more common ground together through interrogating our relationships.

I wonder if we might find in the idea of relationships some ways of discussing human and non-human expertise; some more in-depth discussions of labour, support, and love; some shared language about the enticing aspects of community and the hardships of heartbreak.

Now, I think if you ask Rod (and I know you will), he will probably come back with some response like, "Well, of course it's about relationships, what else do we have?" Or "That's kind of an obvious point there, Dan: are we not all—human and non-human animals—the result of our relationships?" Of course, I don't know this for sure, but I suspect he might say something like that. You can let me know what happens when you do ask him, if you do. My sense is that Rod will offer an interpretivist sociological perspective; one that emphasizes our reliance upon one another, centralizing relationships as a fundamental part of what makes us human. But this last point is an interesting one: how might we explore human *and non-human* relationships in ways that push us together to contemplate our indebtedness to one another? Might an expansion of relationships push us a little closer together, to get through the bullshit limits of distinctions and discriminations? I am wondering about the intriguing things that happen to the categories of "human" and "non-human" when our relationships create new ways of not only understanding the categories but also living within and between these categories. You can see I have been musing while walking. The trouble is, of course, that some of these walks turn into wanderings. And you can easily get lost when wandering.

I just wanted to end by saying that I miss you. Perhaps this reads like a strange thing to say. I know we never met in the flesh. But I do miss how I imagine some of the ways we would have hung out together. Wow, did we have some fun! We were on fire! We caused some trouble and damage, I can tell you. And I miss that fun, even if it is only in my imagination.

Much love, comrade,
Dan xxx

P.S. You're right, the Beatles did bring us together. The love you make, like they said, is equal to the love you take. Relations, Smokie, relations.

Hi Dan,

I have to say that your letters blow my mind, too. And I think you're right—there is a kind of familiarity between us and it seems to have come about in a pretty short time. Know what that makes me think, Dan? It makes me think that maybe that familiarity between you and me was always there. Don't know how that's possible, but it feels like it to me. By the way, did I mention that we—those of us you people call non-human animals—know things mostly by feel? I think that you people, just to maintain the "animal" thing in us, like to call that instinct. It's really a feel, but if instinct helps you people maintain your "human" status, then . . . go for it.

You're right, we were just talking about sitting, Dan. It's very interesting that you brought up walking even though we were just talking about sitting. By the way, Rod did tell me about Ruby and how much walking was just not part of her game. He was pretty happy about this. I didn't know why he was happy because—let me tell you, Dan—when he and I were together, I mean, *together*-together, we walked miles every day; I'm not kidding, miles. Sometimes, we'd be hanging on Bloor Street—you know where that is, you've visited Rod and Tanya lots of times—anyway, when we were hanging around there and then ready to go home, which was three stops on the subway, then a fifteen-minute streetcar ride, Rod would leave the decision up to me. It's true, he would. We'd be walking up from Bloor to the Spadina subway station—know where

I mean?—and when Rod figured we were about twenty feet or so from the door—he was pretty good at judging distance like that, I have to say—he'd say, "Okay, Big Smoke, up to you, babe, ridin' or walkin'? Up to you." Well, for me that was no choice at all. Soon as I heard him say that I kicked it into another gear and we'd "hit it"; that's what Rod used to say—"hit it"—when he wanted to roll. Tell you one thing, Rod and I changed a lot of commands from what the guide dog training school taught us, that's for sure. It didn't take us long to change the command "Smokie, forward," for example. Your blind person's supposed to say this when they want you to go. Rod used to say, "Smoke, hit it," or "Hit it, Smoke" instead. I didn't know what he meant at first, but I liked the sound of it, its feel. Didn't take me long to figure out what he meant.

Had we started writing letters during the first few years Rod and I were *together*-together, I wouldn't have known what you meant by pondering while you were walking. We lived in Toronto for the first six years or so, and it's a pretty busy place. I had no time for pondering while I was walking with Rod (working, as some of you people like to say). I was too busy focusing on three things—first, getting my man to where he wanted to go; I learned that from Ruby. She was *always* mixing up numbers and letters, just for the hell of it. So, I thought I'd do the same thing. Rod told me about it and I couldn't stop laughing for a week—anyway, the second thing I focused on was getting him where he wanted to go safely, and, third, having a shitload of fun moving with Rod. So, you see what I mean; no time for pondering.

Then, that changed. We moved to a little town in Nova Scotia called Antigonish. The two of them—Rod and

Tanya—took up teaching university there at a place called St. FX. And that was the last place I was *together*-together with them. It was a beautiful place.

There, wipe that tear away with my paw; still happens, still miss them.

All right, got my head back in the game. That's what Rod used to say to me when I wasn't focused as much as I should be: "get your head in the game, Smoke," that's what he'd say. So, my head's back in the game. There we are in Antigonish, Nova Scotia. It had a population of about six thousand people—during the school year, though, ten thousand. It was a beautiful town. Lots of fresh air, a little brook running through it, and the sea—I like your word better, sea—close by, lots of swimming, and lots of green space, my God! Green everywhere! I loved it! Of course, Dan, I'm saying "green" for you; I can't see colours, green or not. For me, what you people call "green space" is somewhere where there is very little cement and somewhere where everything smells so much. I mean so much! In Toronto, the green spaces did smell nice, but my nose and whole body didn't get filled up with the smell like they did in Antigonish. That's for sure. And then, the peeing, Dan. I could just pee anywhere, seemed like. That was so nice, too. In Toronto there were a few little green spots, little parks, surrounded by billions of miles of concrete. In Antigonish a few of those spots of concrete were surrounded by billions of acres of green space. Beautiful!

I was getting on by then, Dan. I'd been with Rod, you know, working, for a little over six years by then; that's over forty years for you people. So, it was great not to be as busy as I was in Toronto. I didn't need to focus anywhere near as much. In Toronto I was focused! Even when I was waiting at the street corner with Rod for the light to change, I was focused—watching the traffic, watching the people—once in a while those bastards would step on me—gotta watch 'em, watching everything! In Antigonish, didn't have to do that even if I wanted to—there was nothing to watch. We'd be moving on the sidewalk—Rod calls that pavement now—and I would stop at every curb and wait for Rod to say "hit it." If it was safe, we'd cross the street—that was my decision. Well, in Antigonish—it was always safe. (Here's a joke I overheard someone tell Rod in Piper's Pub in Antigonish one day: There was a four-car collision at a four-way stop in Antigonish one day, took four hours. Get it?) There really wasn't much work on the sidewalk; not too many things to get around, not too many people to get around, hardly anything. So, I would ponder. I'd even look around—look slowly over to my left, then to my right; I have to say, Dan, sometimes I was bored. But the saving grace was that there was so much beautiful stuff to look at. There was grass, trees, and, like I said, that little brook running right through town. It was great. Point is, I would ponder and look around while I was walking. Of course, Rod would notice this. He could feel me looking around in my harness. He was all right with it; all he'd say is, "Come on, Big Guy, head in the game," but he'd laugh when he said this. I think he said it as a formality, just to keep up the appearance that we were a legit, honest-to-goodness guide dog team. We both knew we were a lot more than that.

It was kinda like what you said, Dan, when you go on those long walks: not much to do with a lot of nice stuff to look at—your mind wanders while you're walking. Walking with not much to do was, for me, almost the same as sitting around with Rod or lying down beside him in a bar or restaurant or in a classroom when he was teaching. Not much to do, so your mind wanders—you ponder things, might even grab a couple of Zs.

You said at the beginning of your letter that you and I were starting to get quite familiar with each other even though we have never met—in the flesh, as you say—and only know each other through these letters and through what Rod tells you and through that book he wrote about me. That last stuff aside, though, our letters are bringing us closer, more familiar—it's like getting to know someone you already know. Do you think that's how it always is? Do you get to know those you know, especially those you love, over and over again? There's something about that human/non-human relationship you keep throwing around in your letters that I was thinking about, but, before I get into that, I gotta tell you about something else I was thinking about.

You said that we, you and I, are blurring friendship. You said something about blurring "unacceptability," "informality"—that we were "blurring the boundaries" of friendship. But here's what I think: I think anything acceptable or formal about friendship is what you people make of it. (You probably already know this, Dan, I'm starting to use the phrase "you people" instead of human. You seem to like "human" better, but that sounds a little formal to me—so, I'm gonna use "you people," at least, until I think of something else.) You people decide, usually without even talking about it, what the boundaries of friendship are and then, you say, you blur them. I think they were already blurred; wrapping them up in acceptable and formal behaviour is what made them not blurry, and then you people get all proud when you blur the things you made not blurry. What I think you and I are starting to do together in growing our friendship is to grow the way . . . we see. How mind-blowing is that! I knew lots about you before we started getting to know each other through these letters; Rod taught me a lot about you. Now, I'm putting stuff together. You're not unblurring anything. What I think you're doing, from how I know you, is that at times—haven't figured out when these times happen yet—at times you've got a different kind of sight kicking in. You have that sight, something I haven't seen in many of you people, that sight that sees more than what you people make. There's times—like when you were looking at our friendship, for example—that you see it, friendship in this case, before it's sculpted over by you people—you see it in its blurry glory. You see friendship. But you think you're blurring friendship. You're not. You're living it in its blurry freedom and love. That's what you're doing. You know how sometimes you people say, "something's wrong, it's all blurry, everything I see is all blurry—OMG!" Well, you're different, Dan. You have the sight that sees the blurry of everything.

The human/non-human distinction you wrote about has something to do with blurry. You yourself say that the distinction "seems to lose its purchase." Then you say, "if it had any in the first place." It seems as if you're becoming more suspicious of distinctions, maybe even losing a little faith in them. You say that the movement I was speaking of when I was telling you about some of the things Rod and I did, some of the stuff we got up to and some of the places we went, made you question whether or not this human/non-human distinction had anything going for it. It's funny that you spoke of this as you spoke of movement—Rod, me, he and I moving through the world together. Just as an aside, when we moved—we rocked! We were fast, Dan. Rod loved my speed. He also loved it when we moved in and out of people, especially when it was really busy like on Yonge Street; he loved it when I zipped him in and out, around and around people, cars—you name it. I think it reminded him of his football days—he used to say things like "good job," "nice move," shit like that. Suited me just fine; I loved zipping around those people.

Back to blurry. I'm thinking that in all that movement that Rod and I lived, the blurriness of the human/non-human distinction seemed to fade, if not flat-out disappear. I think maybe, Dan, you were seeing me and Rod for what we were— living beings connected to one another by a bunch of shit—by purpose, by interest, by a joy of movement and discovery, by learning new stuff about the world, about each other—and, most of all, connected in a love and respect for each other's being. That's what I think you were seeing with that blurry vision of yours. You people need those distinctions you invent just to make sure that world of yours stays sensible and has a meaning you always knew it had. I think you people are pretty fussy, too, about which distinctions can hang together, who can take part in this activity, that activity. Who can come into my home and who can't? What do you have to look like for me to hang with you? You people complicate the world with so many distinctions and so many judgements about who even counts as belonging to the distinction of human that it used to make my head spin. What was even funnier is that after you made up a whole bunch of these distinctions and complicated the world, you couldn't figure the world out anymore. You people even get yourselves a postgraduate education with the sole purpose of figuring out the complex world that you people invented in the first place. I got my postgraduate education so that I could mess with you people and guide some blind dude through a world that wasn't even sure he belonged there. Talk about blurry.

I have to clear up one thing: I don't mean Rod and I were and are the same, not at all. But, you can't describe us, not really, as different—that's far too banal as I said in another letter. Rod's distinctly who he is and I'm distinctly who I am. We need that distinction just to hang in the world. But still, the distinction can't be too artificial. Rod tried that, remember? In that book he wrote about me—us, about *us* (that's what Rod always said when I said the book was about me. Selfish academics). He tried to make a distinction between us—remember? He said—nature/society, human/animal—nowadays you people say human/non-human animal—then he said, man/dog—remember all those distinctions? But if you read closely, and I know you do, Dan, those distinctions become harder and harder to see because what you begin to see, if you have your kind of sight, is blurriness. You don't blur the distinctions; you see their blurriness. All the distinctions Rod made up to describe the two of us ended up in one distinction and in one connection—Rod and Smokie, love.

You made me laugh, Dan, when you wrote about how you people, you know, humans, distinguish yourselves from animals. I like the stuff you said about how we feel, you think, we act through instinct, you through cognition—I love all that stuff you said. I got a couple of distinctions that we make—check it out: we enjoy our food and eating, you people ritualize it; we play and fool around until we die, you people want to "grow up"; when we love, we love unconditionally, you people love only if it works out for you; when we got someone's back, we got it forever; you people got someone's back only until it becomes too much trouble; there's a bunch more, but you get what I mean. The most important one for us is that, unlike you people, we are not one iota, not one bit, embarrassed or ashamed of our bodies. Our bodies are who we are! I think Rod was telling me that there was a couple of you people with postgraduate educations that said something like this too.[7] News flash—they ripped us off—it wasn't their idea, it was ours. Unless we're talking to you people, we never have to remind ourselves that we are our bodies—only you people do.

It was interesting to me that you said that one of the things that you people think distinguishes humans from non-humans is that humans "do community" and non-humans "hunt in packs." I think a pack is a community and, from what I heard—figure that out—when wolves hunt, for example, it's a communal activity. They even teach the young ones to hunt. This is just an aside, Dan, something I thought about off and on all of my life: I don't think dogs, like me, are descendant from the wolf. I really don't. It's one of those human ideas that you people have about us and, like so many ideas you have about us, this one is also wrong. On more than one occasion, I've seen one of those little tiny things, a dog that weighed maybe two or three pounds; you tell me how the hell that little thing is a descendant of the wolf. You people just have to stop believing guys like Charles Darwin—although I do like Shrewsbury.

No need to apologize, Dan, for bringing up the issue of "service animals." Now that I think back on it, the guide dog school where I got my postgraduate education operated with the understanding that we (I mean, us dogs) were being trained to be service animals. Nowadays that phrase has taken on a very special meaning. Back in the day, animals pulled wagons, farm equipment, acted as transportation, the whole nine yards. Nowadays if you're a service animal—lah-dee fucking dah. You're helping the "most vulnerable." When Rod and I were moving in the streets of Toronto or anywhere, you wouldn't believe how many times you people complimented me. "He's so smart," "He helps the blind," "He's so special," and like Rod wrote in the book about me, one little kid asked his mom, "Is that one of those blind dogs?" So, Dan, remember—I was some super special kind of dude. Just kidding. It didn't take long after I moved in with Rod and Tanya, Jessie and Sugar, and a few months later Cassis, didn't take long at all before I was a member of that community: not a service animal, just a part of all of our lives together. Still get a tear or two, Dan, even to this day.

I think you're right, Rod and I did produce through our relationship "skills and capacities that pull you both through the world together," as you say. I love how you said, "Your stories are about the possibilities, successes, and outcomes for being in the world produced through your coming together." Beautiful! Not only that, I think you're right—there was something about moving through the world with Rod that was somehow different, I mean, different from moving through the world with my first family, with my guide dog trainer and stuff like that, something different. I'm going to tell you a secret,

Dan—but keep it to yourself—I mean it, keep it to yourself. I don't even know why I'm telling you. Maybe this is another one of those times that you talk about where our friendship is blurred. Anyways, keep this under your hat. Rod tells me you often wear one.

When I first got together with Rod, I had a feeling; it was just a feeling 'cause that's what we do, we feel, unlike you people, who think. I had this feeling and it came about because when I was getting my postgraduate education and dragging blind people around, I wasn't—dragging blind people around. I mean, the trainers were all sighted. Once in a while, they wore blindfolds. But the rest of the time—they just walked around like they could see; that's because they *could*. At the time, I couldn't figure out why they sometimes wore blindfolds. . . . Then I met Rod. I had one of those "got it" moments, those things you people call "aha moments"—now who's feeling and not thinking? Anyway, and here's the secret: I had a feeling when I first met him that Rod didn't like his blind thing; I really felt that. I didn't get that feeling so much at the guide dog school where he and I got some postgraduate education together. We never moved in the streets alone back then; we always "worked," that's how the trainers put it, together, six dogs, six blind people, together. You people are probably confused by this; is it a pack? Is it a community? Six dogs, must be a pack. Six people, must be a community. What to do? What to do? I just love how you people confuse yourselves. Point is, Rod and I didn't work alone, not until I moved in with him in Toronto.

We got home late from the guide dog school; that's when I moved in. It was after the graduation they had—I gotta tell you about that sometime, Dan, it was a hoot. Anyway, we didn't get to bed until late, almost midnight! That was late for me. We were up early the next morning. That's what I do, Dan, I get up early; you know, can't use the toilet inside, gotta go outside. So, Rod and I get up and head out. We wander around the backyard; I sniff around, checking out my new home, peeing my brains out, doing my business while Rod tries to follow me, smoking a cigarette, if you can believe it. He keeps close to me, touching me kinda, so that he knows when I stop and poop, he knows where it is and can pick it up with that inside-out plastic bag. Too much detail, right, Dan? Okay, I'll get to the point.

Right after breakfast, we head out. It was early. I was lying down on the floor beside Rod with my eyes closed, not sleeping, just chilling. I felt him get up from the couch, opened my eyes, and saw him walk over to the door where he always hung my harness. Of course, as soon as he got up, I was up; that's what I do. You never know what the dude is gonna do, walk into something maybe, so I get up, you know, keep an eye on him. He reaches for my harness. Let me tell you, Dan, when he did that and when I heard that little jingle, I couldn't wait to get out the door. I just loved it! It was different moving around with Rod than it was with those blindfolded trainers—it was different. But, back to the secret. Like I said, I had a feeling Rod didn't really like his blind thing. I got that feeling that morning, the first time we hit the streets, just me and him. It wasn't just working, only working, that I loved, there was something about Rod. It hit me—that morning—Rod can't see. He wasn't wearing a blindfold. It wasn't like those trainers back at the school. I noticed Rod doing some stuff that the trainers did when they had blindfolds on. But he didn't have any blindfolds. It hit me—he can't see. And that's when it hit me that he didn't like it. I knew something was up with him at the school; blind, I knew he was blind—that's why we're training, we'd guide blind people. Thing is, it hit me only that morning—Rod can't see! That's what blind means. Can't see with or without a blindfold.

Anyway, back at the school, Rod was on it—Smokie, right; Smokie, left; Smokie, forward—all the commands. He learned them and learned them quickly and loved working—but, like I said, in a community, sorry, pack. This morning—different story—we were alone—me and him—Smokie and Rod—the first time. . . . Forever.

This morning, this first time—Rod was reluctant. He just wasn't on it. I wasn't expecting that. I'd wait for a command from him—sometimes for two seconds. That's too long, to my way of thinking. Let's get on it, be decisive—that's how I like to move. And that's how we did move back at the guide dog school. But this morning . . . it didn't seem like Rod could make a decision to save his life, which, by the way, was the whole point; if he made a bad decision—I was there, saving his life. He was hesitant this morning. It was almost as if he was afraid to move. I didn't know why. The two of us moved like we were wearing rocket boots before, but now it was like he was wearing lead boots. It was strange, Dan, let me tell you. For instance, we got to a curb, I stopped and waited for Rod to let me know which way to go—left, right, forward—which way? Like I said, couple of seconds went by and nothing. I knew he had lived here in this hood for two or three years, so he knew it. So, WTF! What was going on? He knew which way to go, but he acted like he didn't.

Then, it hit me. I mean, I have to say, I felt bad, really bad. It came to me in a flash. Rod doesn't like this blind thing. Now he's got me, all hooked up in a guide dog for the blind harness and I'm guiding him. No hiding anything—he's blind as a bat and everyone—everyone who knows what this harness of mine means—knows it. For a year or so, as I came to learn later, before I entered the scene, Rod moved around as though he were scared to take a step. He was clumsy. Then, once in a while, he'd use that white stick. This made him look even clumsier. He hated that white stick. He used it once, maybe twice, then chucked it. He walked without any guide when he was alone. Man! He tried to hide everything from everyone.

Then . . . me.

Another thing hit me like a flash—I had to make that blind thing something he liked even if only for the reason that I loved it. I mean, what's not to love? I get to get hooked up in this harness, take him everywhere—bars, cafes, restaurants, classrooms, his friends' homes—everywhere. He and I were never away from one another. We were joined at the hip, as you people say. Actually, it was more joined at his knee and my hip. But you get what I mean.

Turned out, I wasn't just a guide, just getting him around. I was moving in blindness with him. Blindness gave me a chance to do shit I never would have done, and I wanted to show Rod that it would do the same for him. One of these days, Dan, I'll tell you about some of the ways we did that. For now . . . still a tear or two.

You're right—blindness does bring beings like me and those like you together. We don't come together, at least Rod and I didn't, in service—but in love. Hey! Just thought of something! "Come together"—he didn't know it, but John wrote our theme song! Rod told you that John was the best Beatle, didn't he?

That morning, that first morning—I knew I had to do something. I wasn't gonna let Rod's blind shit get in the way of taking this city. So, I showed him. I looked both ways and across the street as we stood there at the curb, Rod trying to make up his mind, and I hit it. It looked most interesting over to my right, so I hung a right and hit it. Pretty soon, I felt the bounce in Rod's step, looked over my shoulder and, believe it or not, saw a little smile. I had him. That's when it all started; that first morning—we started—we started to rock the shit outta blindness.

Things just went on from there. At first, I was just happy to work, not like a service animal, but more like what Rod and Tanya used to say—"we're working," and when they said that they meant they were writing. Rod used to tell me about all the work he did when he played football. It was really hard, he said, but he loved it. That's what it was like for me. I loved this guide dog work right from the get-go. When I got home from the school, though, it got even better. I loved working with Rod. I got to experience stuff most dogs don't have a clue about; I've been in subways, streetcars, trains, and even on airplanes a few times. I've been in places they don't let other dogs in; I've been in all kinds of buildings and, oh yes, I've been in pretty much every bar in Toronto, at least the ones in our neighbourhood. I loved doing all that stuff with Rod.

His blind thing gave me a chance to go places, see things, experience stuff I never would have. But the biggest thing it gave me—it gave me a chance to tell Rod, just by hanging with him and working with him, that this blind thing—it can be a shitload of fun. Pretty soon, he got into it and that's when things really changed. Blindness meant more to me than just working and experiencing stuff and it meant more to Rod than just shit. I think that's what I meant when I said we grew up in blindness together. I'll tell you more about this and the fun we had in another letter.

"Heartbreak, abuse, and negligence"—man! You nailed it, Dan, when you said animals and disabled people get treated that way by others. I don't even like thinking about some of the abuse some of my comrades went through—even some guide dogs! And there were a few times when Rod and I ran into some abuse as we moved in the streets. You wouldn't believe some of the shit people would say to us. No one abused us physically. Rod made sure that didn't happen to me and I made sure that didn't happen to him. It was the shit that people said. But when we got into this blindness thing, I mean, really got into it, we found ways to handle it and make the abuse hurled at us act like a boomerang. I'll tell you about this stuff some other time too. I just wanted to say that I liked how you drew a connection between the mistreatment of animals and disabled people—really cool.

You asked me about communicating the world to Rod. I did that, no question. But I did it on many levels. I'm a pretty complicated guy, you know. Like I said, first thing I did was to make sure Rod got to where he wanted to go safely—got him around stuff, made sure no cars hit him, stuff like that.

Then, I started to see the world in different ways than just some stuff to get around. I had a different view of the world than most people did. Remember, you people, unless you're small or use a wheelchair or something, see the world from a much higher point than I do. The world came at me at your knee level, although Rod tells me you're pretty tall, so maybe below your knee level. I did communicate how we were gonna get places to Rod. It was through my harness—mostly. I was in front of him, on his left about three-quarters of my body length. Rod could feel the pull in the harness when I moved and he would follow me; well, one time he didn't and he smacked into a parking meter. I knew he wasn't gonna get too hurt, so I let him do it just to teach him who was in charge—if he wanted to get around smoothly and safely, follow me. Rod wrote about that in his book.

Anyway, that was the other thing I communicated to him—next level of communication—that I was in charge. It takes some of you people a long time to learn that, I'll tell you. Thankfully Rod learned quickly. But every now and then . . . I remember one time we were rocking down Queen Street—block after block after block. We came to many cross streets where there were no traffic lights; so, I would stop, Rod would say "Smokie, forward" when he thought it was safe, and, if it was, that was my decision, we'd cross. After ten or twelve blocks, I noticed Rod was getting careless. We would stop at a curb, he would listen if anything was coming and then, as he said "Smokie, forward," he stepped forward with me. He didn't wait to feel me move, to feel the pull in the harness. I thought, this isn't safe, I gotta do something about this. So, I did. I went a couple more blocks, and then when I stopped at the next curb and Rod said "Smokie, forward" and took a step, I stayed put. The dude almost tripped over his own feet. But he got back on the curb, crouched down, and said, "I get it, Smoke, I get it." I gave him a couple of licks, laughed, and we were on our way—me in charge.

I think the top level Rod and I grew into in blindness together is when both of us started enjoying it. There were lots of times that we hit the streets with nowhere in particular to go. We just wanted to do our thing. I used to love it whenever I heard a jackhammer. That meant that someone was digging up a sidewalk somewhere and there were all kinds of cool obstacles—big wooden planks covering holes in the sidewalk, caution tape at chest level, I mean, for Rod. I'd have to keep my eye out for that because I could go right under it; it was no obstacle for me. But Rod, he would hit it, not that it would hurt him, but he would sure wonder what the hell it was. So, I had to adjust my viewpoint all the time and stop when there was caution tape or even when there were low branches hanging over the sidewalk. Stuff like that—we had fun, I mean, both of us. We also liked bootin' down Yonge Street and Bloor Street during rush hour. It was really busy with pedestrians. We had a lot of fun getting in and out of those people as fast as we could. Don't know why, but we both loved it. Like I said, I think it might have reminded Rod of when he played football. I just loved moving quickly. I remember one time we were in our local with a friend of ours, Gord. Some guy came up to our table and asked if there was a liquor store anywhere near. Gord told him that there was and the guy asked how long of a walk would it be to get there. Gord said, "About fifteen minutes, unless you're these two," he pointed to us, "then, two, maybe three minutes if you have to stop for a light." Rod and I had that rep—we were fast.

I don't know if this is the kind of stuff you were talking about when you were speaking of relationships—"interspecies" and "interdependencies"—relationships between you people and us, humans and non-human animals. One thing I know for sure—Rod and I were close, really close. We were always together; everything he experienced, I did, and everything I experienced, he did. We sort of got on the same wavelength. I got to know when he needed stuff and he got to know when I needed stuff. For instance, he knew when I really had to pee and when I just wanted to jack around sniffing some trees and stuff. Rod was the kind of guy that saw both these things as needs, as something I needed to do. It worked the other way around, too. Sometimes, after Rod had a rough day, maybe some people gave him a tough time for whatever reason and we were on our way home at the end of the day—I would sometimes slow down when we were passing one of the bars we used to frequent—you know, just checking, maybe the dude needed a beer and to chill. There's a lot more to being a guide dog than just getting a postgraduate education.

Rod and I were together—we were a kind of together that was more than just walking and moving side by side. We moved together and, I don't know how to say this, Dan, but it was as though we talked to each other as we moved. Now, Rod actually did talk. He said some of the funniest shit sometimes. One time, we were headed into a building and Rod said, "Smokie, right, find the door." I would always put my nose as close to the door handle as I could and Rod would put his hand down my face, find the door handle, and open it. We came to do this so smoothly that it was hardly noticeable by anyone. Anyway, this one time, this guy held the door open at least five or six steps before we got there. I could have gone right through the door, but then Rod wouldn't have known that. So, I stopped in the open doorway. Rod felt for the handle and, of course, it wasn't there. Here's what he said, get this, "What's going on, Smokie? Is some jerk of a sighted person holding the door open and not saying a word? Is that what's going on? Tell him thanks, Smokie, and let's go in." I swear. That's what he said. Man, we had a lot of fun.

I'll tell you what this relationship business sometimes means to me. You talk about "interspecies" relationships—like me and Rod—dog and man. I get it. What I felt in my life with Rod wasn't that there were two different species hanging together. It was more like something new was made—it could be a third species—I don't know. Somehow we became part of each other. Maybe that's interdependence—interspecies—I don't know. I sure did need him and he sure did need me. And we needed each other for more than just the regular stuff—making sure I had food, water, and me making sure he had a safe trip. We needed each other way more than just that.

He didn't get another guide dog, as you know. I've been keeping an eye on him and sometimes I get worried. He's not moving like he used to. He's quite hesitant, unsure of himself. I hope he didn't go right back to step one in this blindness thing. I don't think so. He's writing a lot about it—seems like. I'm still with him—he knows that.

You're right, when I asked him, Rod said, "Well, of course it's about relationships. What else do we have? That's kind of an obvious point, tell Dan I said so." That's what he said, just like you thought. He also said, "Are we not all, humans and animals, the results of our relationships?" You know him pretty good, Dan. Oh by the way, when he said these things, he laughed his head off. Go figure.

You spoke of how human/animal relationships might bring us closer together and that we might recognize our "indebtedness" to one another. That's a tough one, Dan. Funny thing was, I never felt Rod owed me anything, and I don't think he felt I owed him anything. I think we were grateful for one another and appreciated one another. He gave me a chance to explore the world as a human might see it. I needed to do this to get him around. He also gave me a chance to explore just the kind of things I needed to communicate to a blind person. I loved this part a lot. I think I gave him the chance to rock the shit outta blindness. In fact, I know I did. Sometimes, I think it's more-than-humans/animals coming together; I think it might be two viewpoints, two perspectives, two different ways of experiencing and understanding the world that come together. This kind of coming together makes one kind of funky relationship.

Writing letters to you, Dan—now that's a relationship. Rod's trying, he really is, he's trying to help me say in human terms what I want to say. He learned a lot from me over the years and now I think he's trying to express some of that. He's trying to give you a sense of what I experienced and how I felt when I moved with him and when I lived with Tanya, Cassis, Jessie, and Sugar and when I got to meet their friends. That's what I mean—from my point of view, it wasn't so much we had a relationship as it was that we were together, we were learning stuff and enjoying stuff together. I guess that's a relationship, but not like how humans talk about it. There's no "coming together" in the strict sense, there's just . . . together. We're together—humans/animals—regardless what we think. It's *how* we're together that's important. I think.

Whether or not human/non-human animal relationships can be expanded and bring us more together is an interesting question. Dan, I have no idea. All I know is that there's been a relationship between human and non-human animals since forever, at least since a bunch of animals decided that they were human and the rest of us were not. Most of the time, in my opinion, that relationship was not really good and it's still not very good, most of the time. Non-human animals are always second. It seems that the relationship humans favour toward us is, kind of like you said, we work for you people, provide entertainment for you people, like horse races and dog races and zoos, and, here's the one that always makes me shiver, we're a huge source of food for you people. That kind of a relationship comes from somewhere and I'm sure you know the origin of that stuff far better than I do. It seems that for most of the time all we non-human animals can do is hope that you people treat us, if not with respect and love, at least, well, kindly, what you people like to call humane. We prefer the word "animalane," treat us that way—animalane. Sometimes we non-human animals get a real kick out of what you people do and we have fun copying you—like making up words like you people do. It's fun. I think that before we expand any relationship, we should, first of all, figure out what it is we're expanding. I sure don't want you people to expand cruelty or abuse; that's not a good relationship to expand. This service or work shit is not a good thing to expand either.

I'm not sure I would like the distinction between human and non-human animal to disappear. If we got rid of it, it wouldn't be "we" who did it—it would be "you people." After all, you people have been defining this distinction since forever and it doesn't look like you people are gonna give that up any time soon. There is a distinction between us. I experienced it directly during my life, especially with Rod, Tanya, and the others. Like I said before, it wasn't that Rod and I were different from one another—that's just too boring, banal—but distinct, we were distinct from one another. I felt—because that's what we animals do—feel—that Rod and I were distinct from one another, but we were also the same. Seems silly to feel that, but I did, and still do. In that book he wrote about me, Rod called it "estranged familiarity." He's got a way with words, doesn't he? A real wordsmith. He likes to think that, Dan, so go along with him.

I think you're right, Dan, walking can easily turn into wandering. That happened to me a lot, especially in my later years in Antigonish. It was like I was semi-retired in Antigonish. Loved it though. Still, I'm not sure I want to get through the "bullshit limits of distinction" between us, Dan. I'd like to leave the discriminations, that's for sure. I wonder if intriguing things can happen between what we understand as human and non-human animals "when our relationships create new ways of not only understanding the categories, but also living within and between these categories." Here's a funny thing—Rod and Tanya and some of their friends talk about this "between" thing. I overheard them. To this day, I have no idea what they mean. The only thing I know about "between" is that between Rod and me there's a very special bond. We are connected, no question. Are you saying that we live in our connection? Is that what you mean by "living between"? I don't know if Rod and I live and lived in our connection as much as we *are* our connection. We discovered a whole new world together and I'm not exaggerating. I guided Rod to a place; you know the place—a very special place. He let me guide him into a world of blindness that gave so much to me. It gave me a chance to work, that's true; but it gave me a chance to enter this human world, this world that you people think is so complicated that you made up specialities and expertise to figure it out even though you people made it in the first place. I loved guiding Rod through this world. I showed him stuff, Dan—I showed him how to feel stuff, to touch stuff, to really get to know it. I showed him that there's more to knowing the world than just your four senses—or do you think you have a sense of smell, which makes it five? Can't show you—you have to feel the world. This is where I guided Rod. It didn't take him long to guide me, too. We guided each other into a world of blindness that—and this is what I'm most proud of—he's still exploring to this day.

I miss you too, Dan, and that doesn't seem like a strange thing to say. We did get up to a lot of shit, didn't we? Here's what I miss the most—I miss hanging with you now that you're thinking about all this human, non-human animal shit. What made you go there? Disability? Another thing I miss is that I could have shown you some pretty funny shit that you people get into. I have to say, the all-knowing "human" was a huge source of entertainment to me. Maybe this is one thing I'm indebted to Rod for—he showed me just how entertaining this category human is and he didn't know he did it, at least at the beginning. And you people, you humans, are slow learners, and you're also—Rod told me Rebecca says this and I think it's a blast—"not one-trial learners" either.

By the way, Dan, the most and the best fun anyone ever has is in their imagination.

Aww, Dan. The love you make, it's the same as the love you take. Right there! Right there! We should put that right between human and non-human. Sorry about the long letter, but besides looking after Rod, I really don't have much to do, so . . .

Much love, friend.
Smokie out. Xxx

P.S. I, and the rest of the non-human animals who made up the R and T family, got a lot of presents at this time—toys, lots of treats, bones (both real ones and not real ones), and all kinds of stuff. You people call it Christmas. We call it "bring on the presents."

Dear Smokie. Mi amigo.

Dan in!

As always, comrade, a pleasure to get your letter. It came just before Christmas. An early present no less. I've been reading and rereading. I've taken my time to write. And to be up front with you, I've had my hands full. The better half, or "my life partner" (as they might say in more petty bourgeois areas of North London), has broken her ankle. Poor Rebecca. She will try anything to get out of the Christmas washing up!

I blame you, Smokie—well, I blame us both, really—for all that talk of walking and moving clearly set Rebecca up for a fall! And believe me, it was quite a fall on Rebecca's part. There was a loud "crack" when she went over. And she knew more than anyone that something severe had happened. What a shock. There we were, stranded in the middle of a meadow in North Derbyshire. Four ambulance crews turned up! That's what happens when you go down somewhere so remote. Three nights of hospital. An operation. And then, when she eventually got home, well, we thought, what a shame. We'd been really enjoying the walking together that we'd put in over the year of Lockdown 2020. And now, at least for a while, we won't be doing that together. As I write this she is working away on her laptop, tapping out emails to all and sundry, with her left leg and ankle raised high above her on a mountain of pillows. I'll be back downstairs in a bit to make her another cup of tea. Bless her. It's funny though; Rebecca's predicament and your letter "came together," as the second-most talented Beatle might write, that's for sure. There was a, ahem, blurring of our stories, meanings, and moments. I loved the way you picked up on the idea of blurring—not like a dog who picks up a bone but, rather, like a human who finds a complex idea and runs with it.

You know I'm fucking with you there, don't you?!

Dog with a bone.

See what I did with the old exclusionary distinctions?

Clever, eh; postmodern irony, my friend. Dog. Bone. Jeez, I kill myself sometimes.

I loved the way you are pushing us both to embrace the blurring: to be blurred, to blur, and to seek those blurred moments. Blurring as something productive. Yeah. I like that. I am finding the distinction between walking and sitting to be somewhat blurry today. It seems to us—Rebecca and me—that her walking is over for a while. She is forced to sit. But what's interesting is that we've been talking loads about walking, of trips we've enjoyed over the year and the rambles we have planned for when she's back on her feet. And she's recalled, with an obvious twinge, the day out with the broken ankle at the end of it. *The walk* of Lockdown 2020. The most painful of walks. And the most memorable. It is as if in sitting we have never been more engaged with walking, or at least the idea and promise of it. And these moments resonate with some of the stories you have shared with me about different kinds of walks and walking, especially those times when you were together-together with Rod. What I haven't mentioned about these various walks appear to be narratives of strolling, thinking, and feeling. Let me write to you a little bit about this, if you don't mind, me old mate. You have written a lot. I'm not sure I can keep up with it all or do justice to your text. But I tell you what, at least for now, I'll share some responses with you.

Your stories of the city and town are evocative. I loved the four-car smash gag; nicely done. And I was struck, in contrast, with the pleasure you articulated in relation to the speed of being together-together with Rod back in the day in Toronto (a city that I am sure has a high regard for its residents, wouldn't you agree?). And then, you kept plopping me right back in the midst of this strange place called Antigonish: a quiet, relaxed, and chilled-out backwater set-up. Or "boring shithole" for others. A place, no less, that afforded you the time to reflect. Or as we like to call it over here, "a retirement zone" or "a place you go to die!"

I jest, of course.

It's interesting that you say that you had little space to contemplate the stuffiness-of-stuff when you were caught up in the need for speed (in the happening metropole of Toronto), while you had plenty of time to think when you were in semi-retirement in Nova Scotia. I'm not so sure. I reckon that plenty of thinking and feeling were going on in both places. There must have been many a thought process—and the feel of emotion—when you were negotiating the complexities of the fabulous city of Toronto (God, I love that place). I am wondering, here, if we might want to blur the distinction between different kinds of thinking: reflections (that occur during times of lonesome, sedentary pondering) and flashes of insight (glimpsed in those moments of thought when the world is flashing on by). Is there not a danger of creating a false hierarchy between reflections (big ideas) and flashes of insight (passing thoughts)—between considered and immediate thought? These thoughts about thought (oh, we're getting philosophical) have me thinking about thinking. And, of course, thinking and feeling about being in the world together-together. Do we have to be stationary or sedentary to really think? When we're on the move are we, as I think you're hinting at, rarely thinking? Do you really have to hit retirement in Nova Scotia before you get the time to truly contemplate matters? Do all Canadians hit the coast to reflect on the end of their long lives of movement? How might we blur these false distinctions? Your stories of walking together-together (at different speeds, for varied purposes, across numerous urban and rural terrains) reveal very different kinds of relationships, expectations, neighbourhood conventions, and access to contrasting environments and individuals. While these journeys vary in their speed and intent, all of them evoke intense thoughts. Or perhaps I don't mean thoughts here; perhaps I want to honour the ways in which a different kind of walking and sitting engender *a kind of feel*.

The *feel of* things is a big message that I've taken from your last letter. I loved what you said about instinct being a feel. That's fab. I agree with you. I'm a bit of a fan of old Ziggy Freud, or at least his psychoanalytic stuff around instinct. My take on this is the idea that humans are driven by their instincts for love and death, for joy and devastation. So, instincts are about desires, wants, and feelings. This seems to fit well with your idea of the *feel of things*. This feel is also one of Rod's musings, isn't it? I've heard Rod talk about *the feel* of lots of stuff, including the *feel of* blindness. When you considered the beginnings of your relationship with Rod, you said, "I had to make that blind thing something he liked even if only for the reason that I loved it." You didn't say that you were going to "change Rod's thinking about blindness," or "subject Rod to a comprehensive regime of cognitive behavioural therapy so that he thinks more rationally about being blind," or "tutor Rod in the critical disability studies discourse of how to understand blindness as a product of disabling discourse in the neoliberal machinations of the twenty-first century."

Instead, you referred to getting Rod to "like the blind thing" because you "loved it."

What I read in this was how much you got from the "blind thing"—how it moved you through the world and invited you to connect with others. You spoke of how Rod was not feeling the blind thing; or if he was feeling it, he was finding it to be clunky, frustrating, and full of unwanted surprises. And then you and he started to feel together-together; and this was often smooth, graceful, and eventful, estranged as you were in many familiar ways (you are right, old Michalko was on a roll with that one, brother). I wonder, is this *feeling* truly worth exploring together? And perhaps this is part of the in-betweenness that Rod, Tanya, and others bang on about. Perhaps feeling is the liminal space that cuts through some of the bullshit (human) distinctions that we make in the world:

animal——human
instinct——thought
nature——society.

Take instinct, which you frame as a feeling. Now, through-out our correspondence, Smokie, I've drawn on some tired old distinctions when deploying the term "instinct." One of these is the distinguishing of animal instinct from human cognition. There they are—these categories and dichotomies—like car keys, a four-pack of beer, or the social model of disability (more of that later)—ready and waiting to be used to do their thing. And, like good beer (think the opposite of Coors Lite), they go down so well. Instinct/thought. Animal/human. So the instinct is animalistic (some kind of primeval natural urge), and presented in direct contrast to thought (which is classically humanistic and only ever really owned or enjoyed by the human). Now, your idea of the *instinct as a feeling* cuts through this bullshit.

"How do you feel about blindness?" is a very different question than "what do you think about blindness?" And in honouring the feel of things, then, perhaps we are opening up a space shared by human and non-human animals in precisely the kind of affectively beautiful ways in which you describe your relationship with Rod. Is feeling where human and non-human truly "come together" (as the second-best Beatle once wrote)?

I wonder if that's what you're getting at in your stories of walking and sitting in and across various locations in Nova Scotia and Ontario. It's not that you were feeling more in some places than others, or that the speed of movement meant that you had less time to feel than during those times when you were travelling with less haste. What you and I are doing is laying out various feelings we have had about lives and the accompanying stories that add context and detail to the feel of things. By moving from the stale dichotomy of instinct-thought to feeling-and-thinking, we are able to start really exploring some of the details, highlights, high and low points of our lives. When you pawed away a tear when you wrote about missing Rod and Tanya through to when you exposed the exploitative ways in which humans treat animals, I was with you, because I share your feelings of loss or injustice. You haven't had to convince me intellectually, inundating me with qualitative evidence and statistical findings that empirically support your well-honed epistemologically grounded and ontologically fleshed-out positionality. No. You just, well, *got me*, Smokie. You bloody *got me*. (Excuse me while I too paw away a tear.) I felt those moments with you.

I wonder if *feeling* is an idea, action, or place that we might occupy together as human and non-human animals—in ways where the distinctions between us disappear (or at least feel less important). Might feeling be one mode, element, action, or exchange which builds further the relationalities and interdependencies through which human and non-human animals connect? Might feeling be the in-between space worth occupying, holding onto, perhaps even fighting for? How might we feel together in a space where we have each other's backs?

When you write of blindness, of Rod not liking the blindness thing, and of blindness creating a feeling that one might not want to have, then this got me thinking about the feeling of disability. Truth is, Smokie, I've never really been convinced by a rational argument or a thought masquerading as a truth. Maybe this is me getting older. Perhaps I need to move to the semi-retirement place of Nova Scotia. Perhaps I've become cynical with thinking. But I have always found that an idea has sat with me when it felt at home (that the idea settled in with me). This is not to say that I don't think about disability, or that thinking is not important. You ask me about disability and how I got here. I'll be honest: thinking about disability got me here (or at least in this place called disability studies).

When I found something called the social model of disability, then my thinking was revolutionized.[8] I was able to recognize that my thinking about disability up to that point had been pretty fucked up. While I had members of my family who were disabled, I spent a lot of my time grappling with dominant modes of thinking that suggested people were disabled because of what was intrinsically wrong with them. The social model, on the other hand, was a perspective created by disabled people that shifted the goalposts. The mindset here was that disability was a problem not of people but of society. The social model made a simple though profound point: people with impairments were excluded, marginalized, and dehumanized by society. Note how humanness is used here in proximity to deservedness. And this prejudice and discrimination needed overturning. I thought of my granddad, whose speech was described in terms of a "speech impediment." I considered my nana, who was deaf. They appeared to me to live in a world where their impairments were deemed to be markers of their in-built deficiencies. The social model turned the blame game back on society, on social structures, attitudes, and assumptions that wrongly cast disabled people as problems.[9] Instead, society is messed up and needs changing. I still have alliances to this way of thinking. And I think I always will have this association. Nevertheless, our correspondence is exposing a different kind of need, practice, and desire: to *feel differently* about disability, to *feel differently* about human and non-human animals, and to *feel differently* about our engagements with the world. I think this is what you are describing so vividly in your account: that you and Rod were supporting one another to feel the world differently. And just as you felt blindness then as you and Rod were together-together, you opened yourselves up to feeling blindness in new, uncertain, not necessarily prescribed ways. I was drawn to the ways in which Rod took his infant steps with you in the guiding-together-relationship you began with one another. I read how cool it must have felt for him at the bar when the bartender used your speed of movement in that exchange with the punter. You mentioned how you and Rod "sort of got on the same wavelength." You were getting a feel of the world together—through an "estranged familiarity" as your "funky relationship" grew and grew. I'm not suggesting that no one was thinking here (you don't come up with some punky shit like "estranged familiarity" unless you are cognitively engaged), but I am putting forward the idea that feelings were engendering the conditions for such thought.

So, here we are, Smokie, engaged with the feel of disability and the blind thing. As the best Beatle once wrote, "I've got a feeling, a feeling deep inside, oh yeah." I have to say that I do worry a little about Rod after reading your email. I mean, if you feel it then it must be true. You write, "I've been keeping an eye on him and sometimes I get worried. He's not moving like he used to. He's quite hesitant, unsure of himself. I hope he didn't go right back to step one in this blindness thing. I don't think so. He's writing a lot about it—seems like. I'm still with him—he knows that." That made me feel sad. I hope he doesn't feel he has gone back to step one (whatever that is). I know he's definitely urging me and many others to feel differently about blindness and disability. He's a central provocateur in my life, pushing me to feel again about those matters that I have taken for granted. A familiar estrangement no less. Perhaps you can find out a little more from Rod; check out how he is (you know, if he's still got his head in the game?). I'm sure he has. Probably just needs a steadying paw on his shoulder from your good self. He needs good old "animalane" care!

Animalane—I thought this concept was hilarious. Nice work. I like how you've decentred the human, you old post-humanist you. A word of caution though, Smokie: Rod hates a trendy "post-something" concept. He's often berated me and others for throwing out nonsensical, whimsical, faddy, and fashionable new terms in our writing. So be careful what you wish for and how you use it! But do you think it's about being humane, animalane, or simply finding a way to *feel together-together*?

Over and out for now, Smokie. You've blown my mind enough over the last week!

I hope you feel the love.
Dano.
x

Hi Dan,

Here's a sad kind of coincidence: my last letter to you arrived at about the same time Rebecca broke her ankle, and yours to me arrived at about the time a very good friend of Rod and Tanya's passed away. Mary-Jo—I think her last name was Nadeau—MJ, that's what everyone called her, MJ; she had been sick with a kind of liver cancer for more than five years. She died at home on Saturday, 9th January, a couple of days after your letter arrived. She was only fifty-five years old; that's not even eight years old in my years. Young, too damn young to die.

I never met MJ. She became part of Rod and Tanya's life after they moved back to Toronto from Antigonish in 2006. I knew a lot about her through Rod, of course, but I didn't know her "in the flesh" as you sometimes say. One thing I do know—Rod and Tanya loved her very much—and are really shattered by her passing. Steve, MJ's partner, let her friends know how much her health was deteriorating over the last couple of weeks of her life and that her death was imminent. That doesn't matter. You can know someone is about to die, but, when they do, you're still shattered.

Trust me, that's true. I died of liver cancer, Dan. Rod and Tanya knew I was about to die, but when I did they were shattered. Rod was a basket case for at least two months, maybe longer. I tried my best; but, this death thing, Dan, it's as hard getting used to dying and being dead as it is for those loved ones you leave behind, trust me! Good thing is, I still am around with Rod; we still hang out. I still try to be his guide, but you know what he's like, Dan; he's more stubborn than he thinks he is and—man!—sometimes he's hard to guide. Funny thing is, I love that about him.

I'm paying extra attention to Rod, and to Tanya, too, during this time and so are the rest of us. I'll keep an eye out for MJ, too.

I can't believe what happened to Rebecca! Broken ankle! One thing I do like: if you're going to go down with an injury, go down big! Four ambulance crews! Getting her from the marsh, or from the moors, or from wherever you were walking to an ambulance! To the hospital! Surgery! Casted up! That sounds to me like classic Rebecca—if you're gonna do something, do it big and with pizzazz! You have to respect that, Dan—don't you?

So, more blurring, as you say; this time our "stories, meanings, and moments," as you put it. FYI, Dan—"a dog who picks up a bone" is a dog involved in a very complex activity. I'm not surprised that you didn't know this given that the only time you've seen a dog pick up a bone, or even imagine one doing so, you saw and imagined through that human perspective, that human consciousness, that human way you people have of dividing the world into complex things (human) and simple things (non-human animal). Picking up a bone for a dog is, to use your words, "like a human who finds a complex idea and runs with it." This, Dan, is what you said I did with the "complex idea"—*human* complex idea no less—of blurriness. Funny thing is, you say that when humans pick up a complex idea, they "run with it"—run? Just like a dog? We often do this when we pick up a bone—we pick up a bone and run with it. The other funny thing is that you say that humans run with complex ideas when they "find" one. That's what we do with bones. Unless we're given one by you people, we find one and those are the ones we run with.

You know one of the things I really like about our letters? You "fuck with me," as you say. I do the same thing with you. The thing I really like, though, is that I think you're the one who gives me the opportunity to do that—I mean, to do that right up front without being sneaky. As I said in my last letter, I love fucking with you humans especially when you "find" things that seem to be so mysteriously complex and you don't have a clue that you're the ones who complicated these things. And then you hide the complexity and—this is the hilarious thing—you forget that you hid them and where you hid them and then you're surprised AF when you find them! This is like some dogs—not the ones with a postgraduate education—they bury a bone, forget that they did, and when they find it, like you humans, they're surprised, too. I love people watching.

"Exclusionary distinctions"—I'm not sure what these things are, but they're sure not, as you say, "postmodern irony." I'm afraid I'm with Rod on this one, Dan. The only thing ironic about postmodernism is itself! It says that it "unsettles" the unidimensional, monolithic, grand theory narrative of life, including human and non-human. It speaks of life as perspective, as a whole bunch of them, as multi-perspectives. It also claims there is no Truth. And—here's the ironic thing—it claims this stuff by invoking the Truth of one perspective! Now, that's irony.

Seriously, Dan, you're right, blurriness is productive, as you say. I still have trouble when you say that we—I take it you mean either you people or us—blur things such as distinctions. You say that to blur is productive. I think you're right. But I'm not sure that we, either of us, actually blur, actually do the blurring. We might think we do, but I think that the blurring was already there. Take friendship, which you brought up in your last letter; we could see our letters as blurring the borders of friendship, but I think that we were the ones who established those borders as a way to get rid of the blurriness that friendship came with. This makes friendship safe—we put up borders and we know we shouldn't cross them and, when we do, we say that someone crossed the line, or that we blurred the borders of friendship. Seems to me we drew the line in the first place. I really think, Dan—I really do—that you have the kind of "vision" (I won't tell Rod I used that word) that "sees" (another word I won't tell him about) the blurriness of things like friendship, and that's where you get confused. You think that we need to blur the borders when what you're really doing is "seeing" friendship—just friendship—no borders, just possibility. That's what I think.

I like how you said that walking and sitting are distinctions that are becoming quite blurry for you and Rebecca since . . . the incident. You say now that Rebecca can't walk, and now that the two of you are doing more sitting than walking, you speak loads about walking. Oh, that's interesting. If you speak about walking when you're walking, are you walking? Are you speaking of walking? Or both? You know when you're at a party and you're having loads of fun and someone comes up to you and says, "Are we having fun?" Then, you say, "Yeah, till now."

Like I was saying a few letters ago, because Rod and Tanya are involved in the academy, I've had a chance when we were together-together to listen to a lot of academics talk about a lot of stuff. It seems to me that this is their biggest flaw, their biggest error. They talk about stuff without doing stuff. I overheard one guy when I was together-together with Rod talking about something he called a method for so damn long, without doing the method. Rod told me later, after the guy was gone, that he writes the same way; he talks about and writes about all the stuff he's going to do, without doing it. We guide dogs don't sit around talking about guiding blind people—we do it! Love you academics.

I get what you mean when you say that Antigonish is a "retirement zone or a place to go and die," but it isn't a "boring shithole," as you call it. I know you're jesting and so am I, but there's a ring of truth to it. Everything was busier in Toronto, and Rod and I did work at a much quicker pace when we were together-together there, and thinking about the stuffiness of stuff was much more difficult under those circumstances than it was in sleepy old Antigonish. I did have time to think about things in Antigonish, as I was saying, and I could do this even when I was working. It was a kind of walking that gave me the opportunity to look around, think about shit, stuff like that.

But I think you're right when you say, "I reckon that plenty of thinking and feeling were going on in both places," and that "there must have been many a thought process—and the feel of emotion—when you were negotiating the complexity of . . ." I'm leaving out the part where you say "the fabulous city of Toronto" because, as you know, that'll piss Rod right off. But Dan, between you and me . . .

And then, there you go again, wondering if we "want to blur the distinction between different kinds of thinking." I think it's you people who create the distinctions in the first place—"reflections" as distinct from "flashes of insight." Now there's a hell of a distinction. Thinking, I think, is already one of those blurry activities that becomes either differentiated into distinct categories or blurred even more when we think about thinking. And I sometimes even wonder whether you people, humans, even think at all. Now, I know you do, but I sometimes wonder whether you people think about the different kinds of thinking you do without immediately trying to draw distinctions between them and talk about, as you say, hierarchies of thinking—which thinking is better than other thinking, stuff like that. That kind of thing, seems to me, is more an indication of some sort of agenda at play rather than an attempt to differentiate kinds of thinking. One thing I think for sure is, that kind of stuff, it isn't thinking. It's not instinct either. But it's definitely not thinking. Don't know what it is, but I don't think it's thinking.

Maybe you're right—maybe thinking means something has to come out of it, like you said—time to think gets reflection, thinking on the go gets passing thoughts. I'm not sure, as you say, that all these different ways of thinking about thinking are necessarily false. My instinct tells me, Dan, there have to be different kinds of thinking. When I used to stop at a curb, back when Rod and I were together-together, it didn't seem like I was thinking about it. I just stopped. It was like training, instinct. But when I checked to see if it was safe to cross the street—different ball game. I had to figure out stuff: How far away is that car? How fast is it going? How long will it take it to get here? Shit like that. That's not automatic like stopping at a curb. They are two different things. Whatever I want to call them, they're different and I don't think that difference is false. But you're right, this is getting downright philosophical.

Seriously, though, I don't know, Dan. I think maybe we do need some sort of a time for reflection and contemplation. I gotta check it out, but maybe you're right, maybe Canadians head to the coast for retirement so they can contemplate. One thing I noticed in Antigonish, lotta old dudes sitting around here and there looking like they're contemplating, not contemplating, thinking all kinds of ways. Whatever's going on, there seem to be lots of different ways to do thinking, talk about thinking, and, as you say, think about thinking. I'm not sure I agree with you that these are "false distinctions." Maybe we have to judge distinctions not on whether they're false or true, or right or wrong, but maybe we should judge them on whether they're good distinctions to make. Take me and you people, for instance; there's a distinction between me and you people and I don't think it's false. I can do some things you can't and you people can do some things I can't. I can sure use my nose and ears a whole lot better than even you people with perfect eyesight. You people relied on your eyesight so much, you forget about smelling and hearing and touching. That's what brought Rod and me close—we smelled and heard and touched the fuck out of everything. We sure did. I didn't think the way he did. I don't know what the distinction was, but there was one. And I don't think it was false, Dan. Instead of looking for false distinctions and fixing them up by blurring them, as you say, maybe we should look for good distinctions and try not to wreck them. If we do that, I think we can live in the blurriness that belongs to the distinctions rather than thinking we even have the ability to blur them—ability to blur—is that ableist? I remember Rod telling me about something he read somewhere by someone, don't know who, who said something like the most thought-provoking thing is that we're still not thinking.[10] That's a bitch, huh? I'm using the word "bitch" in your way; it means something entirely different to me, but trust you people to wreck it.

It's like I said in my last letter—something you mentioned in your last one—the biggest difference between you and me, besides that I can use all my other senses better than you and I can run a whole lot faster, is that my thinking is more a feel, what sometimes humans call instinct. I get the feel of stuff, and when I was together-together with Rod I got the feel of blindness—something I tried to teach Rod to do. He's getting there, he's getting there.

I like how you said that instinct, for you people, was about desires and wants, about stuff like love and death, stuff that's almost impossible to think about without feel. I think you're onto something there. I feel, you think; I tried to think, you tried to feel. Now, if that's not a beautiful distinction—a distinction that makes a difference—then I don't know what is. Isn't that a lot better than humans saying that we (non-human animals) are lesser than they are? We have a lot to teach each other about feeling and thinking, the feel and thoughts. Nothing false about that distinction. No need to blur it; it's blurry enough on its own.

I think you're right; I wasn't trying to get Rod to think rationally about blindness when I said I tried to make his blind thing something he liked. But then you lost me when you said a bunch of stuff like "neoliberal," blindness is a "product of disabling discourse." You lost me. I loved blindness and still do, and I was trying to get Rod, as you said, to like his blind thing. You can't do that through the kinds of thinking that goes on in that "critical disability studies" stuff; anyone, if they put their mind to it, can know blindness in this way. I didn't want that for Rod and still don't. I want him to *feel* the blindness, to *feel* that blind thing. I want him to feel it like something that he is, a part of him, and also as separate from him, as something he is and as something that exists without him—this is love. I want him to love his blindness. But I settled for him liking it, at least as a start. I want him to feel his blindness, to feel blindness and not just to know it. I love blindness because I got its feel and that's what I wanted for Rod. It was a project, Dan, and still is.

I don't know much about this liminality thing you mentioned. Lots of people Rod hung out with said that word a lot, but I never really knew what they were talking about. They would say things like "in-betweenness," and "spaces between people and things," things like that. They also talked about distinctions and difference and blurring them. I have to tell you, Dan, I never met a bunch of people so afraid of difference and loving it at the same time. They say things like, "there's a difference between," whatever it is they're talking about, "and we need to blur it." I guess that's a good idea; but there was definitely a difference between Rod and me—maybe that's what those people meant by in-betweenness, a space between

Rod and me. I guess that space, that in-betweenness, becomes whatever we make it.

That space of difference very often gets filled up with all kinds of shit that makes for a not very good difference; look at all the crap that you people put in the space of difference between men and women—that crap turned out to be sexism and, even worse, violence, misogyny, transphobia, homophobia. And there's a lot of crap that you people put in the space of difference between you and us, between humans and us. But you know what? Rod and I never did that. We were so familiar, so loving in our difference. And we also loved our difference. We spent a lot of time there. You know what I think, Dan? I think that's why I can write you these letters—I do.

Here is something else I just remembered that's really great. I heard Rod and Tanya reading some stuff, talking about it; it had to do with Indigenous people and animals. It was amazing! It was about Coyote, kind of a dog, and Coyote could talk! I kid you not! She talked! All the animals talked. Now, that's a great way for humans to see (don't tell Rod I used this word) what you people call non-humans. Not only that, once, get this, Dan, Coyote meets Columbus. What Rod and Tanya were reading was really funny but also a little sad. The other thing is that Coyote and all the other animals took part in creating the world. They weren't just created. Anyway, this is the kind of way I think you people and us can live together; maybe even together-together.[11]

Still, there's a difference between me and you, Dan—there really is. I'm pretty sure we also think differently. I'm more instinct—that "primeval natural urge" you were talking about—and you are more thought—"which is classically humanistic and only ever really owned and enjoyed by the human," as you say. I do talk about instinct as feeling and a feel, but I don't think that cuts through any distinction and I don't even think those distinctions are false. There is a distinction between me and you, Dan, and it's not bullshit, it really isn't. I'm not sure what it is, but it's not bullshit. The only way it becomes bullshit is if we, and by we I mean you people, make it bullshit. For me, the question is not how we cut through the bullshit, but why do we need to make so many distinctions between the human and other kinds of life in the image of bullshit?

I think you're right; if we focus on the difference between human and non-human animals as a difference of experience—how we feel stuff in contrast to how we think stuff—then we can come together. Here's where I think you're wrong, Dan; Paul McCartney did not write "Come Together." The best Beatle wrote it, not the second-best Beatle. But that's just a small point.

Dan—we do live together or, as you put it, occupy space together that has a feel. We feel things about each other and, depending on how this feeling goes, we fill the space between us with all kinds of stuff—with love, with hate, with respect, with who gives a shit, with admiration. . . . And then, we (non-humans) *feel the feel* of how that space is filled while you, humans, think about it. No need to make the distinctions between us disappear—just fill it with good stuff, with love; all you need is love—that's what John always says, anyway.

I like what you said about an idea about disability—how it settled in with you and how you sat with it when it felt at home. As you say, you don't really get that from rational thought. It always seemed to me that an idea coming from rational thought wasn't worth a whole lot if it didn't settle in, if it didn't feel at home. Must be the same with humans because I used to hear them say things like, "Do what your gut tells you," or "Follow your heart." Nothing rational about that.

Let me tell you what this reminds me of. Rod was telling me about how great you are with music, Dan; how amazing you are on the guitar; how you know the words to every song ever written, especially by the Beatles. Rod told me that you had a real musical soul. He did say that you could use a voice lesson or two, but that's just Rod, you know.

Here's what I was thinking—just jacking with you, it's what I was feeling. Having a musical soul is like having a strong and sensitive intellect. A musical soul relies on more than just well-coordinated fingers playing an instrument, and a sensitive intellect relies on more than just a bunch of neurons kicking around. You can train your fingers to play an instrument and, if you work on it really hard, your fingers can play an instrument really well. Same with those neurons; you can train them to kick around in all sorts of intricate ways and, if you work at it, you can come across smart AF. But, without the soul you don't have music, and without the sensitivity you don't have a strong intellect. This is where feel comes in, my brother. You got to feel the music and you got to feel the ideas. Fuck cognition. Get yourself a bunch of soul and a bunch of sensitivity and you got it made in the shade. One problem: how you get a soul and sensitivity—no clue. I have a *feeling* that a soul and sensitivity gets you, you don't get it. Just a feeling.

I'm gonna go out on a limb and do a little bragging here, Dan. I have to be quick about it; they frown on that kind of thing here where I am. If we were together-together, I'd be whispering. You know how I was saying that Rod told me you can remember all the words to every song ever written? Well, he also told me that's all you can remember. He said that he could be talking to you, telling you something, and nine seconds later you'd forget what he told you. My feeling is that it's your music soul that lets you remember all those words, remember what's essential. Who cares about all the other stuff? Who needs to remember all of that?

Here's where I start my bragging. When I first met Rod, we hit it off right away, like I said. One of the things I remember most about him, something I used to laugh at without Rod even knowing I did, was his memory. That dude remembered everything. Important, not important, didn't matter—everything, he remembered everything. That academic stuff he was doing, he remembered quotations, who said it, page number of the book, even the punctuation. But he didn't let that sensitive intellect soul of his kick in and let all of this junk he remembered to settle in with him, move in, be at home. When I started teaching Rod how to feel his blindness thing, things changed. He moved rational thought to one side and let in the feel of the words that other scholars were saying and felt them himself. He can now tell when an academic writes from a sensitive intellect or from the shallow triviality of a memorized vocabulary spewed out as a way to celebrate membership in some sort of juvenile academic club. Talk about bones. Rod now tries—bless, as Rebecca would say—to recognize the ideas that come with a feel—ideas that roam around in the ether looking for a home, looking to settle with a scholar and not with an academic. Those are the most difficult ideas to recognize because they're floating around with a whole bunch of other ideas, ones that don't have a feel, ones that are soulless and are not in search of a home. I came into Rod's life with feel, and he came into mine with intelligence, and I don't think I mean instinct or cognition when I say a feel and intelligence. Don't know what I mean, Dan—maybe you can help me.

I like your story of how your thinking about disability changed when you encountered the social model for the first time. I sure heard a lot about that social model thing from Rod and Tanya once we moved to Antigonish. You said that what changed for you was that the blame game, as you put it, switched from the person to society. The person wasn't deficient, you said; society was, for not making disability a valuable part of it. This is mind-blowing, I got to admit. But you know what else is? What didn't move was how blame and disability stuck together. It's as if someone or something has to be blamed. And, since you people only blame others or things for bad shit, disability has to be bad shit, otherwise . . . what's with the blame game? Sounds like you people need another revolution; I have a feeling that's gonna be a tough go—to revolutionize blame, I mean.

Not that long ago, Rod was going on to me about how he had more explanation in his life than most. He said that he was called on a lot to explain his blindness, but that sighted people were never called on to explain their sight. That reminded me of me. I can't count the number of times Rod was asked by someone on the street to explain me: How does he know when the light is green? How does he know where the subway station is? People asked Rod a bunch of these kinds of questions.

I loved how Rod answered them. He always made up some kind of bullshit and, what I loved even more, is that those ridiculous sighted people bought it. Rod and I had some good laughs, I'll tell you that. Gotta paw another tear away, Dan.

What I was trying to say is that, when Rod told me about this explanation thing, it made me think about blame. Asking for an explanation about why you're blind is like saying, Who fucked up? Whose fault is this? That's where the similarity or familiarity ends, with Rod explaining me, and when the familiarity ends, the estrangement kicks in. "How did that happen?" is something people asked about Rod and me. The difference is my difference was given credit, Rod's was given blame. It's like the social model switching the blame for disability from the person to society; everything changes, everything is revolutionized, except blame. That stays.

I'm still keeping an eye on Rod, Dan. I've never stopped looking out for him; thanks for your concern. I am, like I said before, a little worried about his movement—about how hesitant it is and how cautious. That's to be expected, especially when you start getting a bit older, and, no matter what else it is, blindness is clunky. You have to make it smooth; it doesn't come that way. And smooth is what Rod and I made it for those years we were together-together.

But what I'm most worried about is how Rod is feeling that blind thing. I'm pretty sure he's not feeling it in the same way he and I did—that was something special. What I'm hoping is that he's feeling the creativity and the power . . . at least a little. It seemed to me that he and I created a world when we were together-together. It was like he saw things differently than he did when his blindness was clunky. I sure felt a different world when I was in harness than I did when I was, as you people say, "just a dog." That kind of stuff is power. There are some days, I know, he's not feeling it, but that's to be expected; can't be feeling it all the time. I just hope Rod can keep those days as few and as far between as possible. Of course, I'll help him because "I've got a feeling, a feeling deep inside, oh yeah." Incidentally, Dan—I checked with the legend and he said the second-best Beatle wrote those lines, not the best one.

I'm feeling the love, Dan.
Your friend Smokie.

Dear Smokie,

I heard the news about MJ. Rebecca and I are really feeling for Steve (her partner) and for her family and friends. We said a prayer for MJ. She sounded a very wonderful human being. I would have liked to have met her. I know our Ruby shares a birthday with MJ. Ruby and Steve had an exchange on Facebook intimating that these two strong women would have got on with one another. MJ sounded like a very political animal. From what I read in the dedications to MJ dropping on social media, she definitely lived her political and activist commitments, working with others to think anew about stuff that they may have taken for granted. I was struck by her politics, her commitment to other people, and her sense of justice. I can say that you've done the same for me, Smokie: to think and feel anew. Sounds like MJ would appreciate your kindred spirit; I'm sure you'll be in touch with her. Tell her some guy she never met—but kinda feels he knows her—says hi.

In our correspondence, I have found that you have picked up on some of the words that we've used. I have found myself sitting and moving with some of these words.

Blame is a really interesting one. You write about disability and blame becoming fused together. There are times, it seems to me, when blame does something good in the world. When I think of the ways in which disabled young people, for example, are excluded from their local schools, ignored in their lessons, or treated in less-than-human ways by their teachers, I want to apportion blame. I want to point out deficiencies within the education system: I want all of us involved in education to recognize our culpability. I get angry, imagine conversations in my head that I'd have with the protagonists, the points of order I'd raise, and the triumphant march from the school as the teachers look on with fear. OK, I need to get out more, but it is lockdown! It's funny, you know, Rebecca's sister Charlotte used to be married to this chap who once coined the phrase "the Lawthom finger of blame"—referring to the tendencies of the Lawthom women (Rebecca, Charlotte, and their mother, Anne) to call out a problem. Oh, how we laughed aloud at this one. If someone forgot to pay the parking ticket, put out the dustbins, or forgot a birthday, God help you, for you were to be subjected to the Lawthom finger of blame and an accompanying bollocking. There are times when I think the social model finger of blame needs pointing. The consequences can be really generative: demanding the end of poor teaching practices, getting school leaders to think more about how they set up their schools, urging everyone to contemplate the meaning of education and young disabled people's involvement. After all, how we feel about ourselves will be hugely influenced by how others see and understand us. If you are excluded in school you are going to quickly start feeling ostracized in your own community. I do get your point about the dangers of only ever understanding disability through this blame game. There is a danger that disabled people become passive pawns where very little is said about the feel of disability in the identification of the problems experienced by disabled people.

I think one of Rod's contributions to the disability world—and disability studies—is of a different order. I think he's less inclined to point his finger of blame. Instead, Rod invites people to sit with, say, "the blind thing," or "the sight thing," phenomena that are too often felt and understood already by people when they haven't done a jot of work on revisiting the assumptions and meanings that they attach to these same phenomena. I have found Rod to be generous: He has not necessarily sought to apportion blame when he has talked or sat with others with blindness and sightedness. He has—like you did with him—guided people into conversations and considerations of blindness: to sit with blindness, mess with sightedness, and to play around with both. This means that "the blind thing" is not already wrapped up in some kind of social model language and, instead, is considered and felt together as a phenomenon to contemplate together. But there are times when blame has sat with us in my conversations with Rod and now with you, Smokie.

I have felt the presence of the social model of disability—where the blame game is associated with recognizing the barriers and problems in the world—in our musings.[12] For all our sitting and moving with blindness and sightedness, there is a sense that some things need to be called out. The most obvious one is the presumption of sightedness—in the words we use and the human actions we embody—that are plainly wrong, exclusionary, disabling, or messed up, call them what you want. I've lost count of the number of times in Canada and the UK when a conversation has gone astray because the speakers assumed that we could all see what we were talking about even when Rod's in the room. Here, the finger of blame should be pointed: the speakers got it wrong (and I hate to admit this but I'd be one of those speakers) as we assumed sightedness. So, behind the contemplation of blindness and sightedness is a sense that certain values have to be unpacked and, when we get it wrong, then I feel it is only right to point the finger. Having said all of that, were we to involve ourselves in an endless blame game then I'm not sure if any of us would have the guts to start a conversation at all for fear of being, well, accused. So this is what I think you are offering me, Smokie, in these conversations: a chance to question, to ask, to ponder, to fuck up, to fail, all in the spirit of generosity. This might be the intelligence thing you were talking about, that intelligence is found in those invitations to sit and move together.

This brings me back to MJ. My sense from reading the various tributes, and listening to Rod and Tanya talk of her presence in the world, is that she seemed to embody a generosity of engagement. And this generosity links, I think, to cultivating a sense of creativity and power. You might want to tell Rod that I think he still "has it," creativity I mean. He continues to offer me and many others a space and time to sit and move with ideas, especially about how we are approaching the "blind thing" and the "sight thing." I know he's not interested in blame (well, perhaps he is sometimes, especially when it comes to the question of the best Beatle), but instead he seeks moments of connection, to feel and think. This approach, I reckon, distinguishes him from other "disability thinkers" (or theorists if we want to add an element of grandeur) who might be more interested in the blame game. And this is clearly where you come in, Smokie, in radically impacting on not only Rod's understandings of "the blind thing" and "the sight thing" but also on those of us who have had the chance to read Rod's writing on his life with you. And now this: my very own, bespoke, limited edition correspondence. What a treat. The smoothness that you and Rod exhibited in the world clearly had profound impacts on both of you and—crucially—others that you came into contact with. And this includes me. The more we get into the details, the gifts, the mischief, and the encounters of your times of being together-together, then I find myself not only challenging the assumptions that I hold about "the blind thing" or "the sight thing," but also asking different questions: Why would people do that? So cities and rural towns have a different feel, then? So is Toronto a broken city that hates its people (as Rod's friend, Eve Haque, has said)?[13] What would it be like to live in the middle of nowhere? Why have I been so fixated on animal/human differences? Who knew Rod was so wrong about the Beatles? We start with you and Rod, we ponder blindness, we move through human and animal distinctions (and their blurriness), and end up asking unexpected questions about the world. Perhaps this is what Tanya meant when she spoke of the wonder of disability in her book *The Question of Access*.[14] That if we truly feel and think with disability, then the opportunities are endless.

So, this brings me back to some thoughts on thinking about or feeling disability. I know you and Rod *think* about disability. How could you not. And I take your point about thinking differently (where sometimes this might be related to instinct, training, hanging around too much with academics). And I am struck again by the feeling of disability, the living and messing with "the blind thing" and the "sight thing." There needs to be more time spent with the feeling of our lives and that this feeling is not exclusively the work of humans. I wonder if I have been approaching my questions and correspondence the wrong way around: I wonder if I was seeking answers rather than wanting more sense of a feeling? It's interesting that when disability or blindness turn up in the world, we instantly seek to define, diagnose, and measure. Let's be frank here; that tends to be one of the main practices that we subject disabled people to: diagnosis and measurement. But were we to sit with the feel, then we are engaging with a very different venture or project altogether. Your stories with Rod urge me to consider how we might find love, connection, and affirmation in our engagement with the world. But they also bring me back to thinking. And there might be a finger pointing in the background.

The clearly wonderful MJ was a political animal. And so, Smokie, are you. One could argue that, as soon as you and Rod ventured out of the apartment into Toronto, you found yourself in the midst of the politics of disability. The shape of physical environments and the daft questions of strangers are but two insights into a wider society that is simply not geared up for "the blind thing." While your accounts offer me a feel, I also find myself thinking too, furious with the a priori exclusion that has settled into the infrastructure and the words of others you encounter. When you talk about loving blindness, how might we hold such a feel in a world that seems hell-bent on hating blindness? Indeed, how is it possible to love disability when the environments we encounter and the words we use already seem to despise disability? Am I back to the blame game? Perhaps I am. We cannot separate how we feel from the wider cultural forces that inform how we should and can feel. And, maybe I'm putting too much onus on the human world, but it would seem to me that human beings have created cultures in which some humans (and animals) are deemed more valuable than others. And these human cultures have within them built-in ideas that welcome some humans and exclude others. I am wondering here about how the feel of things gets caught up in the order of things. I am trying to get my head around the notion that any feeling we have is always shaped by the kinds of feelings we are allowed or expected to have. I would suggest that in the human world we are usually not expected or invited to feel disability in a positive, loving way. Disability is the dissing of ability. Disability is often associated with the opposite of ability. And as we know, ability is assumed to be part of being fully human: if you're not able, you're not human. When you write that Rod is finding blindness to be clunky and there is a lack of smoothness (compared with the together-together days), I can't help feeling (and thinking) that any feeling or thought Rod has of his own blindness will be hugely influenced by the cultural ideas of blindness that shape how we are expected to feel. I passionately believe that we have to shift and change the way human beings already understand various aspects of our humanity. When disability studies is doing a good job, then it is creating new, enabling, exciting, loving feelings of disability. When Rod invites a conversation about blindness, he definitely is creating the conditions to think anew together for all of us who are lucky to be around him. And with this invitation comes, I think, a responsibility: to find together new ways of talking and feeling about things together.

And, Smokie, I think that's where you have really made an impact in the world.

Your stories offer many things. One of these is the potency of merging together, the relationships, the in-betweenness, of humans-animals (we can use or refuse liminality here if you want) that puncture some of the already existing human-made thoughts and feelings about disability. I think this is more than friendship, Smokie. This is revolution. I think your stories tell of finding alliances that counter some of the human-made hierarchical cultural assumptions that render such things as disability to be less-than-human. Your and Rod's smoothness, your together-togetherness, not only appeared in the world but pushed against the already-existing infrastructure and attitudes that had disability down as less-than-human. Your more-than-human entanglement queered the pitch: People struggled to get their heads around what the hell was going on. Are Rod/Smokie distinguished as human/animal or human+animal? Are Smokie and Rod, respectively, sightedness and blindness, or something in between? Can the guy see the colour of the light or is that the dog's job? There must be some answers that we'd want to offer here. Messing with the heads of human beings is one way forward (and always fun). But there are also other kinds of answers. And these answers are political, speaking from a position that wants to feel and think of disability differently, aware, as we are, about inequality and discrimination. Some people have called this position disability studies. Some have written theses and impenetrable academic texts that seek to give theoretical flesh to social model bones (try hiding them!). Rod, too, has written in this field of scholarship. It's easy to dismiss academia. Ideas do impact on the world and can have some really positive influences. The social model is but one example. It made the problem of disability a societal one, a human one, and made it not simply the preoccupation of disabled people. If we want to make schools more inclusive, then it's up to all of us to get stuck in. But that is not all we want to say about disability. Human and animal life is so much richer than that which is captured by its failings. There has to be more to life than finding the problem and pointing the finger (though this argument does not work, by the way, if you forgot to take the bins out). And this brings me back to creativity and power: another offering of disability studies (I hope) and a mark of your contribution, Smokie.

At the heart of your stories, as you wrote in your last letter, there is love.

I can only imagine how much Rod misses the together-together times. No doubt feeling and thinking "the blind thing" must be a very different proposition for Rod now compared to when you two were gallivanting around Toronto and the retirement place in Nova Scotia. I can promise you this: I can offer Rod love. And I also will offer him companionship. I want you to know that Rod will never be alone in his feelings or thinking about blindness. But you know that already. You know Tanya. And you know Rod's other pals Rebecca, Ruby, Rosa, Devon, Nate, Radek, Dan A., the other Dan . . . I could go on. And, I have to admit, I'll probably bring out the finger of blame now and again when Rod and I are pondering stuff, pointing at some of the human-made cultural stuffiness-of-stuff that threatens to stifle us all from feeling and thinking more affirmatively about how or what we are becoming. Having said all that, I won't offer to guide him though, Smokie. Do you know how many times I've walked him into a door frame?

Love ya,
Dan

Hi Dan,

Rod and Tanya tell me it's your birthday on Feb. 28th. Happy Birthday, my friend! Rod says that you are still under fifty years old; that makes you about seven. I remember being that age; I was in my prime, quicker than lightning. I flew on those Toronto streets at age seven. Rod had to put rubber boots on my paws to keep the sparks from setting my fur on fire! That's an old joke we guide dogs tell. Happy Birthday!

Thanks for the nice things you said about MJ. From what I heard from Rod, she really did live her commitments to social change and also to friendship; she had lots of those, I hear. I'll check this stuff out more and get back to you.

I have to comment on your use of the term "political animal," can't help it, Dan, just have to. The expression does involve me and, after spending so many years together-together with Rod—well, don't let anything go, that's one of the things he taught me. I think when you people (humans) want to say something that's stronger than human, stronger than being human, you sometimes turn to us, animals. Sometimes being human is just not good enough, especially if you want to say something really rock-bottom, something fundamental, something core. It's like some animals; Rod was telling me about caribou one time, it's like that. They migrate, he told me, and they just can't help it. One day they put their heads up, thousands of them in a herd back in the day when you people, I mean you white people, hadn't destroyed them yet, and said, "we gotta go." Just like that, "we gotta go." They couldn't help it. They had to move thousands of miles; they just had to. It was fundamental to them, rock-bottom; it was their core, their very being. They couldn't help it. They migrated because that's who they were—caribou, migrating animals. So, when you people want to say something about someone who has a strong commitment or passion, or when you want to say something about all of you, something core and fundamental to all of you, you sometimes turn to us animals. I remember way back when Rod and I were together-together, he told me about a book, a sociology one I think, that had the expression "social animal" in its title. It said that you people were social animals. You couldn't help it. You lived together in collectives; we call it packs. It's just at your core to be social. Same with MJ; it was at her core, fundamental to her to be political; that's who she was. She was committed to political and social change. So, because you can't express such strong commitments and passions in human terms, you turn to us, animals. Glad to help you people out; oh, and by the way, you're welcome.

"The Lawthom finger of blame!" I love this, Dan! I hear lots about Rebecca from Rod and Tanya and, I'll tell you one thing, she's one of those humans who's very kind, gentle, and calm. This is what I figured out from what Rod and Tanya told me about her. But here's what I know about people like her. Don't cross them. Never. When people get mad at you sometimes, like when trainers or even Rod got mad at me and yelled at me—big deal. Not only did that not scare me, it had no effect whatsoever on me. But, when Rod said something to me in a very low, very calm, very threatening voice, like "Smokie, never do that again," those words, more that voice, went right through me. When he talked like that, I knew to shape up, like when he said in that calm voice, "Smokie, keep your head in the game." Yelling, screaming, carrying on—that just comes from loud mouths. But, that calm voice—just swallow, take a deep breath and say, "Sorry, of course." I shiver just imaging the Lawthom finger of blame being pointed right at me.

I should tell you, Dan, I had my own version of a calm voice with Rod. When he screwed up, which he did more often than he'll let you know, I would stop, just stop. Here's an example: When we came onto a subway platform, we would move down about halfway and stand against the wall, well, he stood, I sat. I wouldn't move until that train came. No way I was taking a chance of Rod falling into the tracks. He could do whatever he wanted to—give me a command to move, pull my leash, anything—I wouldn't budge. Here's another example: When I wanted something, like if we were walking down the street and I spotted a little park with some grass in it and a few trees up ahead, I'd wanna turn in there, sniff around, have a pee, just chill for a while. When we got near, I would gently move over without Rod telling me to, to let him know that I wanted to turn in somewhere. If he said, "Smokie, let's go," I would just stop. I would very calmly, very quietly stop and not move. He always got the idea. So, watch out for that calm Lawthom finger of blame; that's all I can tell you, Dan.

I think I have to clear up what I was saying about blame and disability. I probably misunderstood you; sometimes you people are really hard to understand. I think it's got something to do with all the words you know, way more than you need. When you said in your last letter that the social model took the blame from the individual and put it right onto society, I had a different idea in mind than you did.

Here's what I had in mind: I was thinking more of the blame we attribute *for* disability—someone or something has to have *caused* it, or else how did it get here? Was it flawed genes to blame for disability? Or was it an illness, a disease? Was it an accident? Or . . . was it the divine finger of blame pointing at the offspring of those who have been horrible people such as, well, horse thieves? That's what I had in mind. I had in mind the fact that all of you people with a disability, like Rod and his blindness, had to be explained. And, after it was explained to you, people who had a disability, it then became your responsibility to explain it to others:

"It's genetic."

"I fell off a bar stool in Nottingham watching the big Red Machine play football, hit my head, and there went my sight."

"My mom stole horses a way back."

Disability has to be explained! Someone or something is to blame . . . for *it*!

I agree with you 150 percent, Dan, that the social model finger of blame should be pointed at the horrible ways institutions and individuals treat disabled people. Whether these institutions are schools, bars, restaurants, cafes, shops, banks, or jerks on the street—the finger of blame ought to point their way. But this version of the blame game blames treatment, attitudes, or policies that are negative and destructive and applied to disabled people. My blame game refers to the explanation of disability in the first place—how did someone go blind? I remember once Rod and I were talking about this when we were still together-together; guess where we were talking? You got it, Dan, in a bar, where else? Anyway, both of us thought it was funny that he had to explain his blindness and no one had to explain their sight. Something had to be blamed for his blindness; nothing was to blame for anyone's sight. *That's* the kind of stuff I was talking about.

Back to the treatment of disability, I agree with you when you say, "After all, how we feel about ourselves will be hugely influenced by how others see and understand us." Of course, disabled students and all disabled people, for that matter, will feel shitty about themselves if they constantly are told that they are shit. Here's where we (animals) and you people are the same; I know a few guide dogs whose blind people are constantly telling them that they're screwing up. Pretty soon, they lose their confidence entirely and do actually screw up because the initial screw-ups were 150 percent the blind person's fault. Whenever a guide dog screws up, it's the blind person's fault. Is that what you people call an unbiased, objective statement? The other thing is, what you said goes the other way around, too. If others treat non-disabled people in really nice ways because they treat disabled people nicely, they, too, feel good about themselves. If you get in with a bunch of people who don't treat disabled people well, like some SPED teachers, and they congratulate each other for being tough on disabled people, they, too, feel good about themselves—but, for the wrong reason!

Here's an idea! Just thought of it! Why don't you people breed SPED teachers like you breed guide dogs? If some-one's a good SPED teacher, make them breeders of SPED teachers. Works for us. Rod tells me you teach at Sheffield University in the UK and he says it's a real big deal; it's made out of red bricks or something or was invented by some guy named Russel. Since you're such a bigshot, maybe you can start a breeding SPED teachers program in Sheffield. What a legacy you'd have! Educators will write about you for centuries! Just a thought.

You were right that Rod doesn't really point the finger of blame when it comes to disability—but you're only a little right. It's true, he does try to get you people to sit with the blind thing and the sight thing. He was already doing this with the sight thing when I arrived on the scene. But the blind thing? I think that was my doing. He did talk about blindness a lot before we were together-together; he wrote a whole book on it—something about a mystery and a shadow, something like that. But he used to be a little distanced from the blind thing, from the blind feel. He had already figured out that blindness wasn't the opposite of sight and that blindness could see sight way better than sight could. But, until we were together-together, the blind feel was just not part of his blindness. I take credit for the blind thing and the blind feel, Dan.

I'm not bragging. That's just not in us. I'm competitive AF, but I don't brag. When Rod and I were training to be together-together at the guide dog school, the trainers would take us out—all six teams—to work on the streets. I don't know why, but I could not stand any other guide dog and blind person to be ahead of us. I kicked our pace into another gear and didn't slow it down until we, Rod and I, were in the front of the pack. I'll tell you another thing, didn't take me long to figure out that Rod liked this, too, except he bragged about it. That's just what you people are like. Funny thing was, we carried on this way when I moved to Toronto with Rod.

You've been to Toronto, you know how many people walk on Yonge Street and on Bloor Street; I nearly exhausted myself from the beginning trying to get ahead of *everyone* whether they had a dog or not! It was like an endless race. I don't think I ever came out of fifth gear for the first two weeks! Rod helped me with this. We were chilling in a little park just off of Bloor Street one day and after I sniffed around and peed about a zillion times—that's what we male dogs do—he sat on the grass beside me, I put my head on his lap and he explained things. He told me that in a city as big as Toronto, it was impossible for us to overtake everyone. Then, he explained to me that most of the people ahead of us started off ahead of us. For the next few weeks, I kept it in fourth.

About this Rod pointing the finger of blame thing, he sure bangs on—that's another UK expression he uses a lot—about you people who do disability studies. Haven't you noticed? It's true, he has some close friends and people he really loves doing DS, people like Tanya, you, Rebecca, Devon, but the others—if he's not flat-out ranting about them, he's making fun, mocking them, laughing at them, all kinds of stuff. Rod's got a bunch of fingers pointing the blame at those people, that's for sure. He points the finger of blame at SPED teachers and rehab people, too, but he mostly disregards these people, doesn't pay much attention to them. I'll tell you one thing, if I was one of you people, I wouldn't want to be doing DS when Rod was around, or if I did, I'd want to be really genuine and thoughtful.

You're right, Dan, about how people, even those Rod knows really well and loves and who love him, do things and say things exclusively in sighted language, things that exclude him! People do that and they did that when Rod and I were together-together. I felt really bad about that. Then, one day I wondered—this is one of the times my instinct kicked in—why people who Rod loves and who love him do this kind of shit. Why? The thing is, when I love, and I think this is true for most dogs, *I love*! There's no conditions on it! My love is what you people call unconditional. I fall in love with you and . . . That's it. I love you, no matter what. You people, though, sometimes are mean AF to those you love! Don't get that. Nope, just don't get it. So, I started to wonder about love and this excluding Rod thing. Then, I remembered one thing that I heard Tanya once saying to someone, might have even been to Rod. She was speaking about this writer that she really loved. Actually, Rod and I went out and got a picture of this woman for Tanya and got it framed. She still has it up on her wall in her study. Lots of people mistake this famous writer for a man; funny, eh. What Tanya was saying is that this woman once said something like how do you love a world with so much shit in it? Then, I thought about Rod and then a question, something like, How does he love a world with so much exclusion in it and how does he love people who exclude him so much? That's what I was wondering. Rod sure loves you, man, I know that.

I don't think it's me who's offering you the opportunity to question, ponder, fuck up, to fail, to glimpse new realities, and to do this, as you say, in the spirit of generosity. I think it's our life together—you people with you people, you people with us, and with others—that gives us that opportunity. Until we make it something different, life is imbued with the spirit of generosity. It seems like you people, and to us you people are famous for this, smack a meaning and a feel on life and smack it hard, knocking the spirit of generosity the hell out of life. Then, amazingly, you figured out what life is, what it is to be human, even what it means to have a body different from our bodies, and then you're at peace.

What gives us the opportunity to mess around with the meaning and the feel of stuff is when that peace is disturbed. I have a feeling, and Rod has a thought, that one huge disturber of the peace is disability. It doesn't unsettle anything, dismantle anything, disrupt anything; it doesn't even crip anything. Disability disturbs; it disturbs. It disturbs the peace you people have created.

You know that guy James Baldwin? You know what he said? I know this because Rod has it written on a T-shirt that Tanya had made for him for his birthday. I also heard Rod talking about this with his friend Devon a couple of days ago. James Baldwin is one of his favourite guys. Right on Rod's T-shirt it says, "The incorrigible disturber of the peace, the artist."[15] Isn't that the greatest thing you ever did hear? And this coming from a Black guy—one of those people who you people used to think, and some of you still do, are closer to us than to you people. If you wanna give us James Baldwin and the rest . . . your loss. Rod and I used to disturb the peace when we moved in the world, your world. It was a funny thing; Rod and I had a world together-together. It overlapped with your world, but it was distinct from it. Our world seemed to disturb your world; your world didn't disturb ours, though; that's the funny thing.

Rod used to tell everyone, everyone, he used to tell them that when we moved through the world together-together, it was artful. That's what he used to tell them. And, you know what? I think he was right. We were artful. He's blind, I'm a dog, and we moved together-together—I really think we were artists and I know through every instinct of my body that we disturbed the peace of your world.

That, Dan, releases that "spirit of generosity" you were talking about. This spirit does result in a generosity of engagement, and it does release creativity and power, just like you say. More than anything, though, Rod and I had fun; we really enjoyed moving through the world together-together. We did all of it; we laughed, we cried, we moved ever so artfully; most of all, Dan—we moved in love. Excuse me, another tear to paw away.

"If we truly feel and think with disability, then the opportunities are endless," as you say, then we'll have to feel its disturbance. Mostly, when artists disturb you people, you tend to ignore them. In fact, you people tend to go stir up the peace you created and, ridiculously enough, some of you people do this through violent means. Keeping the peace through violence, keeping the peace at all costs; some of you people made a peace that isn't really peaceful and—dammit!— you're gonna keep it.

Sometimes I get this peace at all costs thing; it's really hard to let the peace go. It's hard to give up and even to disturb our peace, our taken-for-granted habitual ways of hanging in the world, of knowing it, of counting on it. It's hard to love the artist, the disturber, when it shows up. How the hell are you gonna love blindness? Rod and I used to throw this question around, and I mean a lot. And you're right, this sort of question can't be engaged by you people all by yourselves— you need us. The sooner you embrace the disturbance that is us . . . the better. We create beautiful art, Dan—actually, we're beautiful artists. Next time you see one of us, doesn't have to be a dog, could be a horse, a sheep, and, for you, your two pet cats, Tempa and Florence (Rod told me about them), next time you see us—stop, listen, watch, feel the art. You can do this with disability, too. If you don't do this and if you don't feel the art, then like you say, you people instantly define, diagnose, and measure it. This is how you people create peace. Through definition, diagnosis, and measurement and through other stuff as well, you people quell the revolution of the disturbance, ignore the art and the artist, and return to a life of very disturbing peace. Maybe if you people invite disturbance, invite disability and animals into your world, we might all be able to ask how do we create and love a world with all of us in it?

Here's a question you asked that I absolutely love: "How does the feel of things get caught up in the order of things?" What a question! It does seem, as you say, that the feelings we have are always shaped by the feelings we are allowed to have. And, like you say, in your world, you're not allowed to love disability. Thank God I'm not in your world. I loved Rod's blindness and still do. Why wouldn't I? It gave me a chance to flash my artistry, Dan. I have a feeling that Rod's blindness and all of disability gave you the same chance, and I have even a stronger feeling that you flashed it, too.

I'm not exactly sure how I feel about this able and ability thing. It seems true that in your world, if you're not able (which I guess means if you don't have ability), you're not fully human. I suppose the first thing you people do is to figure out which abilities humans should have, which abilities belong distinctly to the human. Then I suppose that you people figure out who among you doesn't have these human abilities and, together with non-human animals, machines, and stuff like that, you declare them either non- or subhuman. Is that how it works? You people have a whole big huge complex of institutions to decide all of these things. When I heard you people talking about this kind of stuff when Rod and I were together-together, I figured out that you named this huge complex Science. Funny name. I don't know any guide dog or any other dog named Science. Yeah . . . Funny name.

All this stuff about deciding who's human, who isn't, is really sad and not very admirable. And, even though many of you people admire us, animals, and even want to be like us, there's stuff about us that's sad and not admirable. We (not just animals, but all of nature) don't have a great record when it comes to ability either. When we decide who among us is able and who isn't, we don't end up with who's an animal (able) and who is not fully animal (disabled). We end up with life or death. A blind wolf in the wild—not disabled. Dead. A tree crowded out in the forest by other trees and not able to draw water through its roots—not disabled. Dead. A wounded gazelle in a herd—not disabled. Dead. Even I shudder, Dan. Because I spent all of my life (except maybe for the first six or seven weeks) crossed over the border into your world, the human world, I have a little of each in me, some animal, some human. Crossing borders like this, or blurring them, as you might say, fucks with how you feel about citizenship. It's like I had dual citizenship. I was an animal—I felt that world—and I was in the human world. Humans let me everywhere in their world, everywhere—universities, bars, restaurants, airplanes, trains—and when they didn't let me in, Rod kicked up a fuss. He showed them my ID—my harness. Somehow, this proved I belonged in the human world. I had citizenship. Being in both worlds, I experienced the cruelty of each. This tells me, Dan, that there's got to be a whole lot more to this able thing than meets the eye—Rod will get a kick out of that if you tell him what I wrote.

I do feel for Rod. It seems to me that he is experiencing his blindness as clunky, as not smooth, not as smooth as when he and I were together-together. The two of us (the two in one)—we did smooth that blindness thing out. You're probably right, Dan, culture (I guess that's the home of the human) did hand Rod blindness all wrapped up in a clunky way; but he and I took that wrapping and smoothed it out; then, we rewrapped it and that nice smooth wrapping gave everyone a chance to feel blindness, feel its smoothness. Here's the funny thing, though, the thing I like best: even though we smoothed blindness out together-together, we stuck it out in the world—that human sighted world—with its edge of the wrapping flashing. It reminded me of a dream I had last night. I dreamt I was catching a Frisbee. Strange thing—I never ever did that in that other world, the human one. Never. In my dream, that Frisbee came flying through the air smooth as silk, but with an edge. I went after that thing when it was in the air like my eternal life depended on it and grabbed it—right by its edge. I have a feeling that Rod and I—together-together—threw blindness back into the world . . . with an edge. More often than not, the sighted world missed it. Talk about clunky. What Rod is feeling, I feel, is the clunkiness of the sighted world. I just have to get his edge back, Dan—his edgy blindness. I've been doing something about that and I'd like to run it by you, as you able humans say. It involves dreams—next letter, maybe next letter.

You say you want to "puncture, shift, and change the way human beings already understand various aspects of humanity." I feel you give a whole lot to DS, maybe too much, when you say that, when it works, "it is creating new, enabling, exciting, loving feelings of disability." Maybe. Maybe not. I feel one thing for sure, if you want to puncture something with something else, put an edge on that something else. More than anything else, Dan, I think what you say about our responsibility is the best—we have to "find together new ways of talking and feeling about things together." The only difficulty I have is, from what I hear, the new ways some of you people have of talking of disability are really clunky. Got to smooth that stuff out and put an edge on it.

You're right, Dan—we do have more than a friendship and our letters are more than friendship. Like you say, it's a revolution! What else could it be? A dog writing letters to a human, and a human writing letters to a dog. Revolutionary! Not to mention controversial. By the way, the colour of the lights—my job. Rod couldn't see a freaking thing. That's what he used to tell you people who asked. I really laughed hard when he did this, especially when some of you people believed him. He used to say, "I don't know how he sees the lights, he just does. I can't see a freaking thing." Funny AF. Well, I don't see colour, at least that's what you people think. The funny thing—you people just don't get—is that I go by traffic; if it's safe to go, I go; if not, I don't. You people add the colour.

DS has done a lot, as you say. And yet . . . so much clunkiness still exists. I feel—I really do, and I know Rod feels this, too—disability studies has gotten real clunky over the last few years. There seems to be a lot of competition between scholars, artists, and activists, and a whole lot of self-congratulatory activity. DS "folks," as the new jargon now demands, compete with one another for who has more accessibility shit happening, who recognizes more difference, who clunkifies their language to accommodate everybody and everything; who, in short, is a better and more able human being. I remember when Rod and I were together-together, we would sometimes leave a DS talk or activity and nearly slip on all the self-righteousness and moral indignation that dripped all over the floor. I feel that before DS de-clunkifies society's version of disability, it ought to de-clunkify its own. You know what happens when clunk meets clunk—kerplunk.

I know, Dan—I can feel it. Rod has a lot of love. That makes me really happy and somehow a little sad, too. I feel him wondering about things, about his life, about blindness, disability, about how he's lived it, thought about it, acted upon it, and he's thinking, too, about what he hasn't thought, hasn't felt, hasn't acted upon when it comes to his blindness and disability. If there is such a thing as liminality or in-betweenness, that's where he's stuck—right in between having done and having not done.

Sometimes I feel that Tanya, you, Rebecca, Ruby, and Rosa have slipped right into him and have shoved me to one side a little. I know, I know. That's probably not true, but sometimes I feel it. Here's the other thing—you're not supposed to feel that kind of stuff where I am; they frown on it. Mostly, I'm real happy you slipped in. Is it true what Rod says—that you and the three Rs, as he sometimes calls them, live across a body of water that even I couldn't swim? Is that true? Hard for me to believe. One time when Rod, Tanya, and I, really early on when we were together-together, spent a week in a cottage out by a lake somewhere in godforsaken Northern Ontario, I swam out into that lake so far that they had to send a guy in a canoe to get me. They thought I would get tired and not make it back. Can you believe that! Talk about ability.

I can now say it officially, Dan—you're a great friend. I love you. "You say you wanna revolution," the Man said that.[16] You and me, Dan—let's give this fucking world a revolution. Write soon and Happy Birthday.

Love,
Smokie

6TH MARCH 2021

Dear Smokie

My friend. *You say you wanna a rever-loo-shun, well-hell, we all wanna change the world!* What a way to start this Saturday morning in West Yorkshire: here before my computer, writing back to you, reading and rereading your letter, and the voice of John Winston Lennon in the background. You'll know that the second-best Beatle (okay, I'll stop that now) recorded two versions of this song. One was a slowed-down acoustic number (recorded in the key of A for *The White Album*) and the second an electric version that I imagine most people think of as the original (I think it came out as a 45 and was capo'd on the second fret). Enough! My point is that it's one helluva song. And you know what my favourite line is in the song? When John asks if we want a revolution, his response:

Don't you know that you can count me out . . . in.

He was a contrary bastard, wasn't he? I think I'll come back to Lennon later.

Thanks for bending my head. Again. These letters are sure unlike ones that I have written in the past (you know, handwritten ones, pre-email). I can recollect love letters, thank you letters, apology letters, break-up letters, job application letters, Mum-and-Dad letters, catch-up letters. I think a lot of the time I was information-giving, you know, catching up with friends and family, letting them know how I was getting on, perhaps offering an explanation or justification along the way. With these letters, Smokie, they feel like the Marx and

Engels correspondence! You know, two guys thrashing out the foundational ideas of what will become a globally penetrating theory of the human condition! Only slightly joking. My point is that there is a back and forth between us; sharing, disagreeing, challenging, supporting one another. And there is plenty of fun. I don't think Marx covered similar ground. I've always found the lack of discussion of outdoor pissing to be an inherent deficiency within Marxist theory!

I'm glad you rolled with the political animal comments! I knew you'd do something with that. I think your point about the ways in which humans turn to the "animal" to speak of things that are "stronger than the human" is a really interesting one. I read that "social animal" book too, one of the most asocial pieces of writing I've ever read, to be honest. Indeed, what I recall of having to endure that book (it was essential reading in a psychology course I took of which I have zero fond memories) is that it said so little about society. In my last letter I suppose I was trying to work out the ways in which the wonderful MJ and your good self, Smokie, are both political animals.

I was thinking about the impact that you've both had on the world. And one of these is in the register of the political. Clearly, MJ has affected many people through her life, to think in more socially just ways, to connect with those who are marginalized, to speak truth to power. I was struck by the lovely words written by her partner, Steve, about the myriad ways in which she affected others, getting them to think differently about the world and to align themselves with others in search of a better world. MJ sure sounds revolutionary. I'd say similar things about you. You gave Rod new ways of being in the world. As you write, you gave Rod the blind feel which was, previously, not part of his blindness. It's clear to me that you can take credit for that. Over the years you appear to have been involved in a constant process of being together-together, which had many consequences on your two-in-one relationship and on others around you. As I've mentioned before, I knew about you before these letters, not simply through the stories that Rod has shared with me but through the book he wrote about you two. I remember the text really impacted upon how I viewed human and animal relationships but also how it captured the many ways in which your together-togetherness bumped up against the physical and human world which is simply not designed with Rod (and you) in mind. And when I was reading that book for the first time, I was struck by its politics: how it called out the social order and asked us to think again about who is included and who is not. A revolutionary text, no less. So, for me, both yourself and MJ are political animals. And I think that by stating that I'm seeking some commonality, some overlap, a means of capturing some of the work that both of you have done in the world. I'm not wanting to appropriate the animal as a means to extend the human condition; I'm thinking instead of a moment of alliance and of coming together. Perhaps by deploying the idea of political animals, it invites us to think about how humans/animals affect those around us, in ways that might change or disrupt the world.

I say disrupt . . . But then you are pushing me to consider disturbance. Disability disturbs. You say potato, I say potahto. I say disrupt, you say disturb. I've been sitting and moving with that word ever since I read it a few days ago. My initial reaction was that disturbance plays well against the rational, the sane, and the commonsensical. What's not to like! When we find something disturbing, then this feels uncomfortable. But it also can feel uncanny: We are reminded of something that we already feel we know. I wonder if there is a danger that disturbance sits with us primarily within ourselves. It feels like a really . . . hate to say this . . . psychological idea. I can almost feel the psych-lot in white coats with their hands above my shoulders, all ready to pounce and diagnose my disturbed and disturbing thought processes. I can imagine a smorgasbord of talking cures waiting to cure me of my disturbed thoughts and feelings. I'm back in the psych ward. Is there a danger that disturbance settles into these psychological framings, especially in a world that is so obsessed with the psychological?[17]

Now, disrupting has a more material, actionable, and relational feel to it for me. I'm thinking of overturning tables, protesting in communal areas, and flat-out rejecting ideas. I'm thinking of the edgy blindness you and Rod brought together as you enter a bar, classroom, tube train. I wonder if the edginess you describe speaks of its disruptive potential. My concern with disturbance is that it is already known by others who have powerful ideas that circle around this concept. Disturbance is a word that is already reduced by the discourses that circulate around it. I think of disturbance and the psychiatrist appears before me. Disruption makes me think of demolition teams, punk rock, street protests: *rever-loo-shun*. Disruption has a more material feel to it than a psychological one. You might have to forgive me, Smokie; I remain scarred by my psychological training, which seemed to reduce anything of interest to the individual, their brain, and their behaviour. When you ask me to find the edges of things to puncture, then I feel more at home with disruption than disturbance. That's not to say that I am content in my disruption—far from it—nor would I suggest that I necessarily disturb the world in the ways that you describe.

This brings me to James Baldwin. What a human. And what a quote: "The incorrigible disturber of the peace, the artist." Baldwin's legacy is definitely that of the artist. No doubt. But I wonder if this is the impact of the political animal too? And I also wonder what becomes of those of us who are not artists but hope to disturb (or disrupt) nonetheless? I know I have to be careful here when using the "a" word (animal, I mean). As you write, the history of racism by white people is underscored by the association of Blackness with the animalistic and less-than-human. I have to remind myself that all words have many different histories and meanings to them. And putting "political" and "animal" together clearly starts a number of "hares!" But if I sit with the idea of the political (with or without the animal), I wonder to what extent Baldwin's descriptor is something one should only confer upon the artist. To disturb the peace conjures up images of collective and individual protest (as I've mentioned above, I'd prefer to use disrupt, but I'm not going to argue with Baldwin here!). And when protest is effective, society struggles to love a protestor. Does one have to be an artist to disturb the peace effectively? Does disturbing the peace require an artful quality to it? Can one disturb in less artful ways? Are political animals artful in their disturbance?

I am taken by the artful ways in which you and Rod moved in the world together. I read and recognize the smoothness. And I'm envious of it. I don't picture my own life as particularly artful or smooth. I'd characterize a lot of my life as mundane and artless. When I administrate, complete a research grant application, write, or email, I would characterize a lot of these activities as hit-and-miss, ill-thought-out, instrumental rather than conceptual, drab, mechanistic, grab-and-go: all part of a mundane being-in-the-world. Occasionally, I think I might disturb the peace in some small ways. Let me tell you about the other day. I was chatting with some high-profile medics. We had come together around the need for research into healt care, specifically, to find ways we might improve health care for people with learning disabilities.[18] That label—learning disabilities—is the one we deploy over here in the UK instead of horrible old-fashioned terms such as "mentally retarded." We were on a Zoom call (when are we not these days, right?) and a couple of the medics started talking about people with learning disabilities as "service users." This word is a red flag to me. A trigger no less. I butted in. I suggested to them that we could refer to people with learning disabilities as experts, particularly because many of the people I know have been using various services for many years and can tell you very quickly which services are shit, how they can be improved, which services should be dropped, and which services do not yet exist but should be created. To be fair to them, the medics seemed to take on board what I was saying and acknowledged that their language was somewhat limiting and, well, inhumane.

The conversation then moved on to think about the ways in which doctors, nurses, and other professionals could shift their thinking about people with learning disabilities—to assume competence and knowledge. Why am I telling you this? Well, here is one little story from a typical day that involves chatting to medical practitioners about services for people with learning disabilities. I have to tell you, I'm struggling to find the art or the artfulness in this encounter! What I can relate to, though, is your idea of disturbance. My words will not have a huge impact on the medical profession or change the embedded disciplinary views of medics. But, in that moment, I did feel I'd thrown the conversation off course. I think I got them to consider the language they used. I tried to explain a different way of understanding people with learning disabilities. I wanted to explain. I needed to explain. And in that moment, I felt I was doing disability studies. If this perspective, no matter how we understand it, is about disturbing or disrupting typical (so, dominant) everyday understandings of disability, then this was what I was attempting to put into practice.

I'm no artist. But I do think I'm a political animal. I was clear in what I was trying to do: create a moment of critique. I wanted the medics to reconsider the assumptions that they hold about the patients to whom they provide services. I was thinking of the self-advocacy groups that I know—collectives run by people who have learning disabilities—whose starting premise is that they are people first.

I have in mind Denise and Murray, old friends now—people who have survived special schools, endured years of bullying, and fought to be included in their communities. During the conversation with the medics, I was the conduit—the messenger—for their views and aspirations, to be viewed as more than "service users." I recalled times we've spent together where they told me about their lives. Like the time Murray tried to dig himself a hole under the fence that surrounded his special school so he could escape and go back home. I thought of Denise, who lived a solitary, lonely life until she met up with other people with learning disabilities and joined the local self-advocacy group. Do you know she runs a course for medical students now at the university, encouraging them to rethink how they understand disability? There was no artful or smooth feel to my conversation with the medics. It felt kinda clunky. And the stories of Denise and Murray are not redemption narratives; they still have to deal with endless daily moments of prejudice and discrimination. But I do think there are tiny moments of disturbance and disruption, where the peace provided by the normal conventions of medical speak are disrupted by my moment. Where Denise creates space for medical students to revisit their prejudices. Where Murray literally demands freedom from specialist schooling (even if he continued to be educated in special schooling for the remainder of his childhood). Perhaps that was me, Murray, and Denise conjuring the calm power of the Lawthom finger of blame (LFB): to draw attention to the dangerous assumptions embedded in the very idea of a person with learning disabilities! I'd like to think that the late Anne Lawthom—the original creator of the LFB—would be proud. But again, I'm struggling to find the smoothness in these stories. They definitely feel like they have an edge, but I wouldn't describe them as necessarily artful and smooth. But I do think that, at moments set in time, we can consider their disruptive and disturbing qualities.

My worry here, Smokie, is that in searching for the smooth and the artful—in the pursuit of disturbance—we risk ignoring the power of the artless and clunky. I wonder if we are in danger of romanticizing art over other activities (like the seemingly artless contributions of disability studies). Not many of us will achieve the cultural impact or artful qualities of a James Baldwin. Nor will many of us enjoy the smoothness you describe in your together-togetherness with Rod. And, I think, that's okay. Perhaps all of us—disability studies included—can only offer to think and feel with disability. And, like on my typical day, eke out some possibilities in the clunk and junk of the everyday. ("Junk" is a great song by Paul McCartney, by the way.) I'm brought back to John here:

Don't you know that you can count me out . . . in.

I remember once watching an old TV interview with Lennon, who was asked about this contradictory lyric. I recall him saying that the lyrics captured his ambivalence to the very ideas of revolution. At times he was in. Other times he was out. This, for some, could be read as the confused musings of a rich musician. But, while I'm a Paul fan, as you know, I'd like to offer a more generous reading of John Winston O'Boogie (as some of Lennon's true fans also know him). Whether we are smooth or clunky, artful or artless, disturbing or disrupting, disability studies or not, I think that the best we can do is to expose the tensions and contradictions of our lives and those around us. I sense such a feeling of sadness in your account of your time together-together: that you miss those moments. Simultaneously, when you write to me you seem to do so with such smooth clarity and purpose. It seems as if you were so busy getting stuck into the world together that only now you have the space and time to reflect on the lessons from that time in history. I am struck by the celebration of artful smoothness that you describe and the awareness sparked too by living with the mundane. Both the artist and the regular kinda person can reproduce the most sparkling of contributions. What are the dangers of someone placing the artist on the pedestal and the ordinary/every-kinda-person on the ground?

You have demonstrated to me that there seems to be much gained through an interrogating of sightedness and blindness. And while the latter is often explained, the former also requires interrogation, and this discrepancy needs addressing. I cannot envisage (notice all the sight words here) a project of interrogating sight/blindness that would be inherently smooth and artful. I can only imagine a project full of clunk and junk. When you write of "life or death" in the animal/non-human world as a consequence of what we might term as disability, then I am already scrabbling around to find the most appropriate, respectful, comprehensive, and applicable words to understand this sad state of affairs. I'm defined by clunk. My language is useless. I need to work harder to try to write with compassion. In the midst of this chaos, well, I often feel . . .

Don't you know that you can count me out.

You write of Rod, "I feel him wondering about things, about his life, about blindness, disability, about how he's lived it, thought about it, acted upon it, and he's thinking too, about what he hasn't thought, hasn't felt, hasn't acted upon when it comes to his blindness and disability." Well, you can let the old Winnipeg hipster know that our correspondence has filled me with hope that we can find alliances and relationships that endure (even when they moved from reality to the memory of the together-together). And, perhaps most importantly of all, when we open ourselves up to the tensions and contradictions of life—sit and move with them—then it's surprising how much we might find there.

Don't you know that you can count me in.

Love ya, Smoke.
Dan xx

Hi Dan,

"Don't you know that you can count me out . . . in." John Lennon did have a way to express what you people call yourselves—I mean, human. Count me out, count me in; that's the beautiful Lennon lyric that captures the contradiction of being human, and with a contradiction—no less. Brilliant! Here's a funny thing I've been meaning to tell you, Dan; no matter how much they ask him or push him, John has avoided writing a hymn . . . So far. When they ask him, he says, "Count me out." Don't know if he'll ever get to the "in." We'll see.

Of course, you're right, MJ was truly political and genuinely so. Many people, especially in the circles Rod is familiar with, are political, but only for their own self-aggrandizement. They do a kind of political Olympics. Who has more causes? Who goes to more protests? Stuff like that. MJ wasn't like that. She had her heart in the land of a socially just world and her mind in this one, and was unshakably committed and dedicated to attempting to bring these two worlds together. That's political. I like how you speak about politics, saying that it calls out the social order and asks us to think again about who is included and who is not. I think you're giving me way too much credit for doing this. I don't know who I called out and I never asked anyone to think again about who is included and who is not. I just straight up included myself in everything Rod did. Since most of the stuff he did was that human stuff you people do, I just moved right in, included myself no matter what anybody said.

I remember one time Rod and I went to the University of Toronto Press building just off Yonge Street. We were going to meet this guy, Virgil Duff, who, by the way, is also roaming around up here; we were to meet him at the coffee shop, actually a doughnut shop, at the bottom of the eight-storey building. We hadn't been in this building before, so I was really fired up when Rod said, "Smokie—right, find the door." I figured, great, get to see another of those human places. I get Rod inside and find him a table and chair. He liked to sit near a wall in these kinds of places, so I looked around until I saw a table free that was against a wall.

Before I go on with this story, I have to tell you a funny thing. During my postgraduate education at the guide dog school, they taught me (they like to say trained, but I think taught is better) to find an empty chair in a restaurant or bar or doughnut shop. Rod just has to say, "Smokie, find a chair," and I look around, see an empty chair, and take him right to it. What those postgraduate teachers never taught me, though, was that an empty chair at a table for four that had people at it wasn't the kind of empty chair I should be finding. I guess all postgraduate education is lacking. Anyway, Rod and I soon fixed that issue. After the first couple of times of taking him to the first empty chair I spotted, no matter if anybody else was at the table or not, we figured out what to do togeth-er-together. We went over this stuff at our local pub and in a couple of minutes we had it down. After that, whenever we went into a bar or a café or anything, Rod would say, "Smokie, find a table." I'd look around for an empty table, one that

I thought suited Rod, and made a beeline to it before some dippy human took it.

The thing that happened next at the doughnut shop was weird. It wasn't surprising; stuff like this happened to Rod and me a lot, but it was still weird. Rod was just about to take my harness off so that I could relax under the table when the guy working the place comes over and says to Rod that there's no pets allowed. Rod gave one of his laughs, the one that isn't funny. You know that laugh, Dan? Then, he says that I wasn't a pet. He said it through that little laugh of his so I knew he was just jacking with the guy, so I gave Rod's knee a nose rub to let him know I knew what was going on. Rod told the guy that I was his guide dog. Then, listen to this, he says, "He's my eyes." I gave Rod three or four nose bumps when he said this, hoping I could make him laugh. Rod does this a lot. When one of you people used to say ridiculous things about me or about me and him, Rod would say ridiculous things back at them. Usually, they got it and apologized. But this guy, thick and stiff as a brand-new harness. He just kept insisting that Rod and I had to leave; "No animals." That was the policy.

Usually, Rod would just ignore something like this, sit and order something. He would usually say something like, "Bring me my order or call the cops. Your call." This time, he hooked me back up and told the guy that his "joint," that's what he called it, "wasn't civilized enough for a well-educated and well-read guide dog team." When we got out of the café, both of us nearly split a gut laughing over what just happened, especially the "well-read" part.

We went through another door, went up the elevator to the University of Toronto Press offices. Virgil Duff met us at the reception and wondered why we weren't downstairs in the doughnut shop. When Rod told him what happened, Virgil got quite angry. We went right back down there. Virgil found us a table and said that he would be right back. He was back in a couple of minutes. About thirty seconds after that, the guy, the thick one, comes over and asks us what we want. Of course, Rod couldn't leave it alone, so he says to me, "Learn how to read the menu yet?"

We had a great time. Rod and Virgil spoke about a manuscript Rod brought to him and I had a great rest under the table. Oh—everything was on the house. The thick dude didn't charge us.

Whether that was a political act or not, I don't know. I think you're giving me too much credit, Dan. I was just happy doing what I was doing. I loved Rod, loved Tanya, and loved the others. I loved moving everywhere with Rod, being with him 24/7. I didn't just guide him around; we did it with pizzazz. We had fun, adventures, and we must have broken every guide dog rule in the guide dog postgraduate education reading list. Not only that, when people asked about us, about guide dogs, about blindness, Rod would always make up some kind of a story. I'm guessing that to this day there are people in Toronto who have got the weirdest conception of guide dog teams in the world. Maybe that's political, Dan; maybe that's political.

When you say that MJ is a political animal, I don't think that you're trying to "appropriate the animal as a means to extend the human condition." It probably is more an alliance or a coming together, as you say. I'm not sure, though, that "political animal" is a way to invite people to think about the human/animal relation. I don't think that such thinking would even disrupt the world. I think you need us. Nothing complicated. You need us. What makes it complicated is that sometimes you people just don't like to admit that. Think about it, Dan. Sometimes you people have a great deal of difficulty speaking of things such as unusual strength, incredible commitment, extreme passion, unrelenting dedication, unconditional love, stuff like that. These sorts of things, although human, sometimes feel to you people as not human. They seem more animal, and there you have it; you need us. MJ's dedicated, relentless, unconditional commitment to the exposure and eradication of social injustice is human, all too human—more animal. You need us. How's that for a disruption?

Speaking of disruption, Dan, I like how you drew a distinction, or was it a binary, between disturbance and disruption. You say that disturbance "plays well with the rational, the sane, and the commonsensical." The binary you create is that, although you say you hate to say it, disturbance is more psychological than is disruption. It only makes us uncomfortable and lives inside of us and is uncanny since it brings something to our attention that we feel we already know. I see where you're getting this from. You people usually, and in a common-sense way, use the idea of disturbance as something up with the mind. When you people meet someone who is not like you or who does things that are beyond human comprehension, you often say that they're disturbed. So, I get why you think disturbance might be psychological. I think that's the rational, sane, commonsensical part of disturbance.

You say that in contrast to disturbance, disruption has a "more material, actionable, and relational feel to it." (It seems to me that everything is relational, but we'll leave that one . . . for now.) I laughed when you said disruption reminded you of overturning tables, loud protests, and the flat-out rejection of ideas. That's great.

Just because disturbance is "already known by powerful discourses associated with abnormality and normality." Really? What isn't? Of course, as you say, disturbance is surrounded by these ideas, "powerful discourses," that circulate around it. Still, I can't really think of anything, even language, that doesn't circulate in the middle of the ebbs and flows, the smooth water and rapids, the calms and the storms of the circulating culture. Demolition teams, punk rock, street protests—revolution! This, for you, is disruption! I love this, Dan! This is why you say disruption has a more material feel to it than disturbance.

Here's a thought. I was thinking of disturbance more like Baldwin does, disturbing the peace. There is something loud and noisy and even material about punk rock, demolition, street protests. But there's also something peaceful as well. These sorts of noises are quite easily covered by the peaceful categories of freedom of speech, diversity of cultural expression, human stuff like that. I'm thinking more of disturbing that peace. We can give a psychological read to anything. But you probably know this better than I do. Since I was together-together with Rod, and even now that we are together, I hear all kinds of human stuff that frames street protests, punk rock in a psychological way. I wonder if this isn't one reason, a big one, that so much of this noise hasn't changed anything. Well, that's not quite true. But I like how you people speak of social change when it comes to racism, sexism, even ableism;

you people often say, "Things are much better now, but we've got a long way to go." This always makes me and Rod laugh.

Here's a funny thing, Dan; I don't think Baldwin was defining the artist when he said, "incorrigible disturber of the peace, the artist." I think he's describing features of the artist. The artist is not a peaceful kind of dude, I think he's saying. The peaceful conventions of society always find a way to either put down disruption, fold it into its customs and norms, or adapt disruption into a relatively new set of customs and norms. Disturbance—will have none of it. The artist is incorrigible in this way. Try not focusing on "disturber" and "artist," check out where that gets you. What could it mean to be "incorrigible" in the face of "peace"? All of us say we want peace. Yet, what is it that we want? What is peace? I don't mean this philosophically, I'm not that kind of guy. Do we want to be at peace with ourselves, with our world? Does Rod want to be at peace with his blindness? Is the world at peace with his blindness? Sometimes, Dan, sometimes I think Rod's blindness is disturbing, sometimes even incorrigibly disturbing. When this happens—art. Blindness becomes artistic, artful—the incorrigible disturber of sight—blindness, the artists. I just made that up, Dan!

I don't think that there is a negative dichotomy such as a binary opposition between disruption and disturbance. I don't even think it's a matter of—what do you people call it?—semantics. It's not a matter of semantics or pronunciation. Rod was telling me about this one time that he and Tanya were in Philadelphia. They were in this shop where there were things to buy with Philadelphia written on them. Tanya found a coffee mug and read it to Rod. It said, "You say tomato, I say fuck off." He and I laughed about that. It reminded me of that time when some guy in a café in Toronto came up to Rod and said something like that's a really nice dog guide, meaning me. Rod told him that I was a great guide dog. The guy got a little edge and said that the term wasn't guide dog, it was dog guide. You put dog first, not guide, and he stuck to his guns. Rod called me DG for a while after that. He pronounced it "Deege." Anyway, this is a long-winded way for me to say that we don't have to make disturbance and disruption enemies.

One of the reasons you seem to like disruption more than disturbance is that disturbance raises all those psychology memories for you and they're bad memories, as you say. That's the same sort of issue I had with Rod when I first got together-together with him. He had all sorts of memories about what blind meant. Of course, like your memories of psychology, his memories of blind were what that massive bunch of you people, what you call society and culture, told him blind was. I don't really know what other guide dogs feel, but I feel my job is way more than guiding some blind guy around so he gets to places he wants to go without getting hurt. At the heart of what I do—did—here comes that tear again—was guiding Rod away from the blind he had into a blind we were making together-together. That's disturbing.

If you disrupt something, it usually fixes itself and goes right back into place. Disturbance is another story. You might try to fix it like you're a psychologist trying to fix a disturbed mind, but it's always there; it stays; disturbed minds haunt us. Blindness is like that, Dan. It's disturbing. Some people say blindness disrupts sight.[19] But any disruption can be adjusted, rehabilitated, some of it even cured. Blindness disturbs sight.

Once that happens, you can't go back to looking and seeing the way you used to. Maybe all disabilities are like that. Disturbing.

Rod was telling me about how you took a bunch of people, people with learning disabilities, on a trip somewhere on a train. One story really stuck with me. He said there was a woman, one of the people with a learning disability, who made her way into the first-class carriage. She sat in a seat that belonged to a businessman with an ill-fitting suit and a briefcase. He didn't know what to make of the woman with a learning disability. That was disturbing. When she left, he was left with a briefcase and an even more ill-fitting suit. Nothing was disrupted. There was nothing for him to fix. He was disturbed. I betcha he still is. That woman and her learning disability come together-to-gether, and in the first-class carriage, they came together as the artist—the incorrigible disturber of the peace.

There's nothing more peaceful than normalcy. It was like that with me. I was a normal puppy—just playing, running around, eating and drinking stuff I shouldn't have been, just having fun. Then, they stuck a harness on me. WTF! Then, they taught me—in postgraduate school—to drag blind people around. WTF! They let me play and stuff like that, but there were rules. Lots of them. Then, I slowly started to figure out that this blind person named Rod I was dragging around, when he came to the school and stayed for a month, I started to figure out that he couldn't see anything! Then, I figured out I had to keep this guy safe! Without me doing my job and focusing, he could get killed! First, I figure out the guy can't see, and then I figure out I'm responsible for him. Talk about disturbing.

When I moved in with Rod, Tanya, and the others in Toronto, after the first little while of guiding Rod around, somehow we arrived at the conclusion that we should do this guiding thing like it was more than just guiding. I knew I had to take Rod into a whole new world of blindness and he knew that if he was gonna follow me into that world, he was gonna do it with pizzazz, grace, and he was gonna do it artfully. And that's exactly what we did. I thought Rod and I were damn good artists. We disturbed a lot of sight and a lot of sighted people. And we did this artfully. But, after I heard about that woman with a learning disability on the train, I'm thinking there's gotta be a lot of artists around doing a shitload of disturbing . . . artfully.

Sometimes, Dan, I think that disturbing shit is a little bit like the Lawthom finger of blame. It's not loud and noisy. But when you see it pointing quietly at you. . . . The woman on the train wasn't loud and noisy either but . . . Thank you, Dan, for saying that I'm a "political animal" and a revolutionary. If I am, I'm part of the "quiet revolution," I think. I stared down a lot of sighted people when I was together-together with Rod. I'll have to tell you about that someday.

Try not to "remain scarred by your psychological training," Dan. Disturb it! Do what I did with Rod and his blindness; take your psychology into regions that will be disturbing AF. Don't disrupt it. If you do that, it'll be like Rod was with his blindness—letting it scare you and letting it keep scaring you. Be incorrigible. Disturb the peace that psychology is and that so many people find in it. Be an artist, Dan. Somehow I have to remind Rod to be an artist and not fall back into the blindness . . . he was.

You're right, James Baldwin was an artist and some of us are not. But Baldwin was speaking of peace in a way that needed to be disturbed. There's lots of kinds of peace, I guess. The peace you people find in normalcy is one kind and that's the kind that Baldwin seems to want to disturb. I don't feel that if you want to disturb the peace and become a revolutionary, you have to become an artist first. I feel that what Baldwin was telling us is that wherever you find the peace being disturbed, you will find an artist doing the disturbing. That's the challenge. You can't disturb the peace unless you're an artist. This means that if you're disturbing the peace you're an artist, but only if you're incorrigible in disturbing the peace. Disrupters move the pieces that make up the peace around, sometimes a little, sometimes a lot. And this does result in social change, sometimes a little, sometimes a lot. Disturbing the peace doesn't move the pieces of the peace around. It punctures peace. It damages—forever!—the peaceful feel we have in the peace that is normalcy. Don't draw artificial distinctions between the artists as they are conventionally known and the artist of which Baldwin speaks. You, Dan, are an artist. The sooner you fess up to this, the better.

You said that most of your life was "mundane and artless." From what Rod told me, you created a conference, which, BTW, disturbed the fuck out of conferences, centred on the mundane and normalcy. Theorizing Normalcy and the Mundane, you called it. You should've called it Disturbing Normalcy and the Mundane. After all, that's what you do, Dan. And you're incorrigible! Time to get a beret, Dan.

The thing that disturbed the peace the most since I've been connected with the world is the Black Lives Matter movement. It really disrupted things too. Everything got disrupted—traffic, businesses, schools, everything. All regular ways of doing stuff were disrupted. But the most revolutionary thing was the disturbance it caused. Even those white supremacists, even they were disturbed by how many people of colour were out protesting. Those people, especially those red-neck Republicans, found it disturbing that all those Black people and people of colour would be out on the streets saying that their lives matter, and those Republicans were also disturbed by some white people supporting BLM. All those white liberals who thought things were getting better for people of colour, but there was still a long way to go, were disturbed when all those people of colour said—now! Right now! Now is the time to go that long way! Basically, it was very disturbing for white people to realize that other lives matter, not just theirs.

Rod was telling me about a documentary that he and Tanya and some of their friends were watching, one you recommended. It was about a camp for disabled people and protests at Berkeley for disability rights. Same thing—disturbing. True, things got disrupted, but it was disturbing for all those able-bodied people to come face to face, even on TV, with disabled people saying we're part of this society, we're part of you. That's disturbing. I think you're giving Rod and me too much credit. We did disrupt a few things; people had to change how they talked to us, even Rod's friends, making sure that I was included. They knew I had to leave a bar from time to time to pee and that Rod had to ask the waiter or waitress to bring me a little bit of water, stuff like that. But, once in a while, we disturbed the peace. Unbelievable as it is, Dan, once in a while, people would ask Rod the most ridiculous questions.

"Do you know where you're going?" some guy asked Rod, and this wasn't the first time it happened. Depending on his mood and how much of a rush we were in, Rod would either stare the person down until they slowly backed off and walked away or he would say, "No. Where the fuck are we?" Or "No. Do you know where we are?" Nothing was disrupted. But the peace that came with the certain knowledge that blind people, even with guide dogs, knew nothing because, after all, seeing is knowing, was disturbed. Rod and I should've been charged with disturbing the peace a whole bunch of times while we were together-together. I think we need both, Dan—a loud disruption of things and the quiet disturbance of the peace.

I thought that was a pretty funny term for people with learning disabilities that those medics you were talking about used: "service users"! WTF! Who doesn't use services? You said all of you were on a Zoom call. Weren't all of you using the service of electricity? I like how you told the medics that people with learning disabilities who use services presumably designed for them are experts and can tell you which of these services are shit. I'm glad the medics thought their own language was "somewhat limiting and inhumane" after you explained that people with learning disabilities can tell them which services work, which need to be dropped and changed. I think you did disturb them, Dan. You gave learning disabled people a label that they, the medics, thought they had, even owned—expert. What was disturbing for the medics was that labels are not now nor were they ever the problem; the type of label was. The label learning disability and other more inhumane ones are a problem. The label expert is not. Funny how that works. One of the difficulties with calling disabled people, learning or otherwise, experts is that the conventional experts then use their expertise to rationalize their own expertise and the disabled experts don't get paid and, if they do, not anywhere near the conventional experts' rate of pay. We need to think of another label for "disability knowledge" than "expert."

You said this medic story was just "one little story from a typical day." Told you you were a disturber and incorrigible to boot. You disturbed the peace that the conventional conception of learning disabilities gave to those medics. They were the experts, and learning-disabled people were what they were expert in. You disturbed this peace. It would have been hilarious if the woman from the train was with those medics. After she left, those medics would have been very disturbed as they walked away in their ill-fitting white lab coats. You said you were having trouble "finding the art or the artfulness in this encounter"—look in the mirror, Dan, the metaphoric one. In that image you will find the incorrigible disturber of the peace—Dan, the artist. If you look very closely into this metaphoric mirror, you might even see the image of the woman on the train. How artful is that?

The search for smoothness; that's a damn good search, Dan. Let's be smooth AF and rewrite something that Rod told me a DS friend of his wrote—nearly every culture should view disability as an opportunity to search for smoothness.[20] Can we put that on a T-shirt? Bumper sticker? Coffee mug? Can we tattoo it on medics' foreheads? Dan—you are as smooth as that glass in the metaphoric mirror.

I think you're right, the search for smoothness might ignore the artless and the clunky. You're also right—DS is artless and clunky, for the most part. You're also right, not all of us can be James Baldwin and not all of us can attain a smoothness, especially an obvious one. But, along with DS, we're all artless and clunky. I think even James Baldwin would have said he was. Most people, even Rod, think of blindness as clunky and even artless. And most people, and even Rod, are right—blindness is artless and clunky. Here's where the search for smoothness in disability cuts in. Here's where not only thinking *with* disability, Dan, but *how* we think with it is crucial. It marks the beginning of the search for smoothness. How beautifully smooth is Jeremy's artless and clunky activity of digging a hole under the fence to escape the normal treatment of his learning disability? How disturbing and artistic is that? How disturbing is it that those people who not only think of themselves but believe themselves to be normal never take up the artful clunkiness of digging a hole to escape their normalcy? Jeremy now has a tunnel and he can move freely between the world of normalcy and the world that normalcy has never even glimpsed. How disturbing is the peaceful smile on Jeremy's face as he moves back through the tunnel into the world of normalcy, where he grabs another clunky hunk of normal and brings it through the tunnel with him into a world that will certainly smooth it out? And how disturbing is it to know that the first thing that hunk of clunky normalcy confronts at the other end of the tunnel is the metaphoric mirror image of the woman on the train? How smooth and artful is that?

How poetic am I?!

Exposing the tensions and contradictions of our lives and of the lives of those around us may be, as you suggest, the best we can do. I sense some sadness in what you are saying here—as though you feel strongly that you should be doing more than playing around with the junk of everyday life, as you put it. That's how Rod used to feel about his blindness, Dan—a bunch of clunk and junk that he had to do his best with. I want to remind you, like I reminded him, that you people have created many art installations with clunk and junk. There's the ones by official artists (the ones you differentiate from the non-official ones) who make sculptures out of clunky stone and junky metal. And then there are the artists who take the clunk and junk that resemble home: clunk and junk such as bits of tents, sleeping bags, cardboard boxes, and fashion a tent city in the middle of a city like Toronto or New York, an art installation to homelessness and poverty. Like the sculptor Henry Moore, these homeless people are the incorrigible disturbers of the peace—they are artists. They do disturb the thin veneer of economic vibrancy a city understands itself to be.

In our time together-together, Rod and I did experience the contradictions and tensions of his blindness and I tried to convince him not only to expose them to the world, but to himself as well, and I tried to convince him to keep these contradictions, to live them, and one day, hopefully, to love them. There's a word that you people call ableist in this next quote, but it's a line from a song by Kris Kristofferson that Rod used to play a lot when we were together-together and I really liked it:

> He's a walkin' contradiction,
> partly truth and partly fiction.[21]

The truth about blindness is a tricky thing; so many of you people have your ideas about what it is. I'll bet you those medics you were talking about know the truth of blindness and so do those educational psychologists you work with. Rehab people, people on the street, everyone knows the truth about blindness—even Rod. He says it's clunky junk. How true is that? How true are all of these truths? Here's what I feel: What every truth needs, even truth about blindness, is a good story, the more fictitious the better until blindness becomes known as a living contradiction, partly truth and partly fiction.

Rod and I were stuck into the world together, as you put it, Dan, when we were together-together. It was a lot of work. We were focused, very attentive to our surroundings; we concentrated on differentiating between what was crucial and what was a distraction; we negotiated innumerable obstacles, including you people; and there were the obstacles of both beautiful and bizarre interpretations of us that we had to negotiate. "Stuck into the world" is a good way to put it, Dan. And yet, at the bottom of everything and surrounding everything was our journey—mine, Rod's, ours together-together into the world of blindness. Stuck as we were in the sighted world, there was that other world, a world, I realize now, only Rod and I knew. We did bring some of it into the sighted world, but mostly it was our world. There was so much stickiness and so much of life between two worlds—there was fun! And a lot of it.

I think you're right, Dan, it's only now that I can check out our time together-together. I think it's the same for Rod, although he did write that book which was a reflection on our life together-together while we were together-together. I told him then, and I still believe it now, he should've named that book—*Smokie*. That's all—*Smokie*. I have what a lot of you people really love and some of you people even imitate—one name. Madonna. Cher. Sting. Prince. Pelé. Come to think of it, these would be great names for guide dogs—don't you think? I think we do need some distance from our lives in order to reflect upon them. But I think it's possible to do that even when we're living that life. Either way . . .

The great thing about the artist as the incorrigible disturber of the peace is that we don't have to put up with the way you people insist, and incorrigibly so, to build hierarchies. You ask: What are the dangers of placing the artist on the pedestal and the everyman on the ground? I would respond with another question: What do we call the artist who is not on the ground? Maybe that's a riddle, not a response. We should think of some answers to this riddle, Dan. Lots of you people say that art is in the eye of the beholder. Sighted shit aside, that gives a lot of artfulness to the beholder. On the ground, the everyman, the artist; sometimes I feel that these three entities blend into a beautiful, not always pretty, artful, and artistic perception of the life that you people built together and the life that you people built as a way to include us, me and Rod—this last thing is sometimes one of those not-so-pretty times. A blend is always a better option than a hierarchy. BTW, Tanya says this about red wine.

Sometimes I feel that we're all defined by clunk and junk. But, like we say up here, one guide dog's clunk and junk is another guide dog's art. I don't think your language is useless, as you say. It can only be so if you think of language as something instrumental, as something to be used for something else, for expressing thoughts or feelings, for example. But what if we thought of language in a different way and not as an instrument in service of something else? What if you people thought of yourselves as different from language users, service users?

The cool thing I learned about language when I was together-together with Rod, and even during my postgraduate education, was that it was a beautiful way to work out communicating with one another. My postgraduate education led me on a path figuring out how I could figure out WTF the blind person meant. Then, when Rod and I were together-together, we developed a language. We blended all kinds of stuff together and came up with a language. But we didn't do that just to communicate; language wasn't just for that purpose, for us. It was how we came together-together, how we fell in love, how we got to be what Rod described by that clunky term "estranged familiarity." Language was who we were and . . . still are. Rod was telling me about when he could see, not a lot, but some, that he saw a painting—I think it was called the *Mona Lisa*. He said that her smile was mesmerizing. How beautiful is that language! The really beautiful thing is that most of you people have the language of the smile. Even I learned that language. I'm speaking it now as I'm feeling my way through this letter to you, Dan. There's so much art on the ground. You people don't need to put select artists on a pedestal. It's just your habit. And habits are hard to break. That's why the legend wrote, "Don't you know that you can count me out . . . in." The only way that's not a contradiction is if it's partly truth and partly fiction. Which it is.

Alliances and togetherness; I really feel what you're saying, Dan. There's so much to experience in our tensions and contradictions when we experience them together, in alliance, as allies. Rod always counts you in and now, so do I.

Almost forgot, I need to warn you about something, Dan. That book you wrote where you just counted "human questions" in, the one where you wrote about the woman on the train—that's what I need to warn you about. You better get to it and write something, something really poetic, something with compassionate language, something titled *Woman on the Train*. If you don't, I warn you, Rod will. You know what he's like, Dan. As soon as he gets an image of something he loves, he won't drop it. To use an expression you used a few letters ago, he's like a dog with a bone. By the way, we dogs have an expression for such tenacity: he's like a dog with a harness. So, write something—quick! Rod has that image of a woman on a train and I can see it, I really can; I can see that image growing in his head, in his heart, and pretty soon . . . What I'll do is have a talk with him, I'll have a word and that'll give you some time to get on that train, the train with the woman on it. Hurry—and mind the gap.

Love you and have a blast on your fiftieth revolution around the sun—now, that's a revolution.

Peace out—I've always wanted to say that.
Smokie

Dearest Smokie,

Thanks so much. I needed your words today. Things have been difficult of late. I'm finding this pandemic thing all a bit too much. I know I have to check my privilege here. I'm not shielding myself from the outside; I get out to ramble around the countryside every day. I've got a job. The vaccinations are rolling in the UK. There are people in far, far more difficult places. But my place, home, well, it feels like the walls are closing in. Every day feels more confined. Days slip into nights. Weekdays and weekends feel the same. Shit, I'm sure Rod is feeling it too, and Tanya, and those two have it far worse than me; they're stuck in a busy city that hates its people, for Christ's sake! So, your words were just what I needed. They hit home.

"I think you need us. Nothing complicated. You need us."

I'm not sure about the lack of complication (I think we both know this stuff is never simple) but "you need us." I'm taken by this. I'll come back to this. But for now—the disturbance/disruption debates of 2021! In time, they will become known by future generations of students and scholars as "the disturbance/disruption wars" of the early twenty-first century. Screw Žižek and Peterson.[22] Forget your alt-right and liberal culture wars. This is where it's at, baby; the infamous Goodley and, er, Smokie debate (I never asked about your second name), an intellectual duel to end all intellectual duels! OK, I know we are both lovers, not fighters, and I think we're dancing around the same kind of ideas, but I want to respond (at least a little). You'd expect nothing else.

Do we want to be at peace with ourselves, with our world? Does Rod want to be at peace with his blindness? Is the world at peace with his blindness? Sometimes, Dan, sometimes I think Rod's blindness is disturbing, sometimes even incorrigibly disturbing. When this happens—art. Blindness becomes artistic, artful—the incorrigible disturber of sight—blindness, the artists. I just made that up, Dan!

Maybe, as you write, we are getting tied up in semantics here. One person's disturbance might be another's disruption. But I must tell you, I'm still uneasy with disturbance. I don't want to labour the point (which is a line people use before they, well, labour a point), but I wonder if disruption has a more external, extended, distributed feel to it than disturbance. I want to keep disruption because it has a less psychology-friendly vibe to it. You write that things that are disrupted can be easily fixed, while disturbance has a more persistent, perhaps resistant, quality to it. I'm not convinced. The thing about disturbance is that it is an entity that suits some of those who want to keep the peace. That's my problem with the supposedly most human of perspectives, psychology. Disturbance is not only tolerated by psychology, disturbance is something engineered by psychologists. And this multi-billion-pound industry of psychologists and psy-professionals (okay, as I've told you a zillion times, I tend to exaggerate) who use disturbance as an object of inquiry and intervention. Disturbance is *the* site for reparation and rehabilitation. Disturbed people and disturbing minds are vaunted as the very things on which psychologists can prey and, by extension, maintain their power. Give me disruption every day. I have a feeling that disruption is not as easily psychologized as disturbance. I'm thinking of the coffee mug in Philly: You say disturbance, so says psychology.

My concern with disturbance is that when it is named, measured, or recognized, it's often in service of keeping the peace. The peace of normality. Psychology loves its normals, of course, but also uses disturbance to reflect back on where normal can go wrong. And disturbance is permitted to sit at least on the edges of the normal. Disturbance is tolerated. Disruption feels more subversive—less easy to pin down—and reaches out to others in its practice of rupturing the taken-for-granted. Disturbance is readily invited in by the status quo. Who really gets pissed off with a little disturbance? And those who are disturbed, well, they're the bread and butter, the lab rats, the paying clients, the subjects of psychology. Disturbance seems to have really been owned by psychology. I am not convinced that we can reclaim a phenomenon that has been so filled with the stuff and nonsense of psychology. I worry that disturbance is already so known, monitored, and patrolled by psychology and other sinister forces that it might have lost its radical purchase in the world.

Now, disruption, well that feels less easy to pin down. Disruption has an edge to it that makes it less easy to be pulled into a recuperation of the very discipline and disciplining of psychology. Your beautiful accounts of the Black Lives Matter protests and your reflections on *Crip Camp*[23] reveal their disruptive brilliance. Disruption leads me out of psychology—a place that I will never consider home—and into the school and the street. Kids that disrupt classrooms. Black lives that freak out white privilege. Blindness that disrupts sightedness. Together-togetherness that disrupts the isolating consequences associated with the usual tales of blindness and disability. Now this, my friend, is disruption. I'm not being pedantic (or should it be engaged in pedantry?!). I just don't get the same sense of excitement from disturbance as I do from disruption. Might this be a symptom of COVID-19, I wonder? Am I reaching out for something that feels like a radical break with the everyday? Is it the psychology or, at least, the pains of living life as a recovering psychologist?

All this talk of disturbance/disruption, potato/potahto; perhaps we are talking across each other. Or maybe we are talking to each other but mixing our "Ds." I love the ways in which you are seeking to break the peace of the everyday, when that mundane and ordinary is shot through with some of the most pernicious and dangerous of ideas and assumptions. I salute your incorrigible disruption/disturbance. What brings us together, Smokie, is a sense of unease with the ways in which the taken-for-granted just seems to roll on by as if untouched by others. The commonsensical stories of blindness. The reasonable narratives of disability. The regular accounts of whiteness. The untroubled feel of the normative. The peaceful vibe of the status quo. We clearly need our disturbance and disruptions more now than ever.

The stasis of everyday life—which I think might be one explanation for me feeling so down just of late—incubates a kind of lazy acceptance of the reasonable and the regular. This peace that you describe is of course only really experienced as peaceful by some of our fellow human beings. Animals too, as you have written, are often forced out of these supposed zones of peace and tranquillity. Any entity that disturbs or disrupts the peace is always rendered undesirable. And this talk of peace gets me thinking not only of feel but also of place. You write: "At the heart of what I do—did—here comes that tear again—was guiding Rod away from the blind he had into a blind we were making together-together. That's disturbing."

On rereading your last letter, I was struck by a recurring theme. Of journeys. Of routes and destinations. I wonder if we were all getting so worked up in our own talk of disruption and disturbance that we were missing something more important. And then you came to me with tales of travel. You disruptor. Have you found us yet another way of thinking together about our interconnections, of our mutual engagements, of our shared animalities/humanities? Have you offered us another route through which to answer the very questions that kicked off these letters and the considerations that we have revisited together over these last few months?

Journey is an overused word here in the UK. I blame British pop culture. I am sure you haven't done this—you strike me as far too cultural for this, Smokie—but I've spent far too many hours over the years watching reality TV programs. Some of these programs—sorry, shows—are dedicated to finding the next big pop star, chef, or entrepreneur. They go by names like *Pop Idol, Masterchef,* or *The Apprentice.* Regular folk are chosen to join these shows with the promise of fame and fortune. Cameras follow these poor people around during their everyday lives, grocery shopping, rehearsals, shows, and demonstrations, culminating in a panel of judges choosing (or not) to save them from the axe. At regular moments, the viewer is rewarded (if that's the word) with close-up intimate interviews with each of the contestants (for that is what they are now) and they are asked what winning the show would mean to them. Without fail, fear, or hesitation, each and every one of them speaks to the camera and earnestly tells us that becoming the next pop star, chef, or businessperson would mean the world to them because "I don't want this journey to end now." That stuff kills me! "Being on a journey" has become *the* way of describing one's aspirations, desires, and ambitions. God love 'em. I've watched so much reality TV shit that I am sick of hearing about life being a fucking journey.

Until now.

There is no doubt that you have set Rod on a wonderful journey. From what you have told me, it seems that Rod had been travelling blind down a number of familiar routes. These well-worn roads are also well travelled by psychologists, rehab specialists, and the usual special ed suspects. It strikes me how many people, devoid of special ed training, find themselves following these roads, all leading to the same place. A particular and familiar destination. A place that already, apparently, feels it has captured the meaning of blindness. Perhaps, to keep with the focus on song writing, we might call this a "Town Called Malice" (with thanks here to the Godfather of Mod, Paul Weller, and his post-punk band The Jam). Imagine this place. It's a dystopian location, populated by residents, some professionally trained, others not, all holding onto ideas of blindness that are dressed up in the language of deficiency, of lacking, and of less-than-human. There are psychologists here, of course, speaking in Freudian tongues (others are available), eager to diagnose, to know blindness in ways that they already know. This is a place at peace with its conception of blindness.

It knows blindness. Not sure what kind of disturbance or disruption is going to shatter this status quo. Perhaps this Town Called Malice is beyond saving. Journeying to this part of the world will only end in tears.

But you, well, you guided Rod down a different path toward another location, a blind you were making together-together. Let's call this new context Nottingham, in order to capture this locality's beauty, magnificence, and, in honour of one of its famous sons, *moi*! I wonder if we were missing the point—or the road—during our debates about disruption and disturbance. Your stories of together-togetherness offer up new cartographies, directions of travel, and new places in which to settle (for a while or maybe longer). You write: "I think you need us. Nothing complicated. You need us." Your letters have shown me that I need you to guide me down new routes toward new destinations. Just like Rod needed you. I appreciate you mentioning the story from the train. As you know, this was a story of a group of people with learning disabilities—a People First group—on their way via British Rail to a self-advocacy conference in Edinburgh, Scotland.[24] The story said something about the wonderful chaos of our journey:

> The train finally pulls in. We frantically
> make our way onto Coach C. Bags are located
> on the luggage shelves by the already stinking
> WC. Elizabeth, Jackie, Asif, Ken, and Peter [as
> with others mentioned in this book, I deploy
> pseudonyms] occupy their seats around a table.
> The train pulls off, shaking us violently from left to

right. I check our party's seats to ensure they match their reservations.

All good.

But I'm not good at this. Disorganised and chaotic is how my friends describe me. They're not wrong.

One of our bags had been left on the floor of the coach.

A female passenger trips over our abandoned luggage.

"Fucking hell, who put this here?" she asks, pulling herself to her feet.

I apologise and drag the bag under the table.

The train sets off.

Where's Jackie?

I panic.

Is she still on the platform?

Ken reassures me. No, she definitely got on.

I push through the automatic doors into the adjoining first class coach. Jackie is relaxing in a seat that has clearly been reserved by an officious looking business chap in an ill-fitting suit. He is trying to explain to Jackie that she has taken his seat reservation. Jackie smiles; ignoring his pleas.

"Jackie," I explain, "You're sitting next to me in the other coach."

She stands, takes her handbag from the pull-down table, and follows me down the coach. Business-man looks relieved. He has his space back to himself. He tuts, shakes his head. He throws his laptop onto the table in front of him in that careless manner of people who have money.[25]

I shared this narrative in the book to show how the group, in their own way, disrupted the normative spaces of the carriage and the peace of the train. But now, as I think about your guiding of Rod to a different place where blindness might be known differently, I wonder if I missed the point of the train journey. Elizabeth, Jackie, Asif, Ken, and Peter were on a different path, with a very specific destination in mind, a place where many people with learning disabilities were getting together under the banner of self-advocacy. Once we arrived, Smokie, I got to tell you, it was fantastic. New friends were made. Sore morning headaches were made in the bars of the night before. Conference sessions were led by self-advocacy group members. Professionals were slated for treating people like children. Services were hammered for failing. Alliances were created that exist to this day. Delegates decided not to take their psychotropic drugs those days of the conference. The conference began and ended with a reaffirmation that self-advocacy groups were coming together from across the UK to fight for their human rights, to demand disability services to sort their shit out, for "staff" (the preferred word over professional) to assume competence and capacities on the part of people with learning disabilities. Revolution indeed. And the journey and the destination were, to use your words, really about those self-advocacy groups guiding one another away from the place "that they had" into a place "they were making together-together." "I knew I had to take Rod into a whole new world of blindness and he knew that if he was gonna follow me into that world, he was gonna do it with pizzazz, grace, and he was gonna do it artfully." Poetic indeed. You reminded me of another poet:

> Two of us sending postcards,
> writing letters on my wall.
> You and me burning matches,
> lifting latches on our way back home.
>
> We're on our way home.
> We're on our way home.
> We're going home.[26]

Paul's song. Recorded late at night in Abbey Road with John. Just them. An acoustic guitar and a bass. If you listen carefully, during the second verse, you can hear them laughing at the end of one of the lines. Pure joy. Together-together. On their way home. You write "at the bottom of everything and surrounding everything was our journey—mine, Rod's, ours together-together into the world of blindness." This journey into the world found you and Rod enjoying and enduring various terrains and settling in certain locations. Some good. Some bad. Some by the sea. Others in the midst of cityscapes and cosmopolitan hipsterdom. I'm struck by how you write about a place of comfort, grace, art, and pizzazz. This world of blindness created together-together. I felt that, too, at that self-advocacy conference in Edinburgh, with Elizabeth et al. The tacit knowledge in the room. The sense of connection and possibility. And it was bitter/sweet. What we were experiencing together in that place at that time was so different to the train and our experience of stares, fear, annoyance, impatience of some of the commuters. The journey had its challenges. But we got there. And Edinburgh felt like home. In your second letter to me you wrote: "I guided Rod for nearly ten years and, when I say I guided him, I mean everywhere—all around Toronto and then later all around Antigonish, Nova Scotia. We took subways, streetcars, buses together, travelled on trains and even planes. We did everything together. This sounds like a lot of work to humans. In fact, you humans call us working animals, or even worse, service animals; I hate that name. I loved hanging with Rod, taking him to all the places he wanted to go and even to some places he didn't."

I'm finding home a bit difficult these days. Mostly, I long to be here. But more and more I feel agitated, unsettled, distracted, and impatient. I want to be taken to new places. I want to get the hell out of Dodge, baby. Our correspondence has permitted me some precious time, every couple or three weeks, to imagine together with you the promise of new destinations. As I read your accounts of travel and guidance with Rod, you so kindly invited me into your space of together-togetherness in which we might imagine new ways of being together. Where blindness and disability are not already known but are imagined together on a journey. God, I am one of those reality TV folk.

I don't want this journey to end.

Your and Rod's ever-moving journey through and with blindness, the encounters with sight, the bumping up against those who feel that they already know, those many moments of joy and humour (even in the midst of antagonism and closed-mindedness), speak to me of the dynamic nature of our interrelations with one another. My earlier preference to deploy clunky distinctions of animal/human or disability/ability now simply does not work in this more fluid and imaginative sense of life as travel. And I realize that I don't even need to leave my home to move. In our correspondence I'm struck by how mobile we can be through our imaginings and imaginations as we jet off to different places, to destinations we want to go and even to those places that we might not. The never-ending potential of travel challenges the static, fixed, and seemingly immovable ideas of blindness and disability that threaten to pull us back. Your movement with Rod in your together-to-getherness makes me feel and think blindness not in terms of prescribed diagnoses or prognoses. Instead, if someone were to ask me about blindness or disability now, well, I think I'd tell them about (your) stories of bar conversations, negotiating a choice of chairs with walls to rest upon, pissing in parks, smoothness of travel in and out of subways, comedic one-liners in response to daft questions, descriptions of cute babies, animalities and humanities, and postgraduate guide dog education. I would perhaps talk about James Baldwin, Black Lives Matter, a conference in Edinburgh, John, and Paul. I'd no longer seek to define blindness or disability but, instead, I'd recount tales of travel, people, and locations. But I have to tell you Smokie, I don't think you should talk in the past tense of your times together with Rod. They are clearly part of the present. You and Rod are still moving, still exploring, still bumping into people. Your together-togetherness remains an incorrigible disturber of the peace (there you are, I gave you your disturbance!). Your direction of travel is still unknown and it's never over. And while you might not be together-together as you were before, in this imagination you have created with Rod and all those you come into contact with (including me), you are more than alive, more than human, more than animal. Is this the art you have in mind? To be more than alive?

I began my first letter to you by stating that "one of my main regrets in life is that I never got to meet you in the flesh." I don't feel this anymore because you have given me one of the most precious things that one could give to another: the chance to travel and imagine together. And what a gift. To be able to luxuriate in the possibilities of imagination and to not know where you might take me next is a wonder to behold. I wonder if this is where our animality and humanity converge: in the possibilities offered by wandering and wondering together?

Thanks, Smokie.
With love,
Dan

P.S. John L. never wrote a hymn? FFS, have you listed to "Imagine" recently? Xx

9TH APRIL 2021

Hi Dan,

Thanks for your letter. It's always so great to hear from you. I suppose you're right; this could be the last letter, at least for now. I like your proposed title for all of the letters—The Disturbance/Disruption Debate. More on the debate theme later. For now—COVID-19.

I don't think that you're the only one who's "finding this COVID thing all a bit too much." From where I sit—I do a lot of that, Dan, sitting—this COVID thing seems to be too much for all of you, for all of humanity, for the entire human race, for . . . Do you people still think of yourselves as a race? I don't know exactly what to call you people. Maybe I'll stick to "you people." This COVID thing has you people everywhere, all around the world, really messed up and scared AF. Can't blame you. This COVID thing has already killed a few million of you and made a bunch more of you really sick, so being scared is not such a bad thing.

Another thing I've noticed—from where I sit—is that this COVID thing has got you people fighting with each other again. Who caused this COVID thing? Who started it? Whose fault is it? Who should we hate? You people seem to always need someone to blame. Can't blame you for that either. (Where does the Lawthom finger of blame point?). Trump has his own idea of who's to blame. The Chinese. I hear he even called it the China virus. After that, everyone ramped up their discrimination toward Asians. From where I sit, that kind of discrimination seems to be everywhere.

Then there's the fight over who gets the vaccine. Who gets it first? If that wasn't bad enough, it seems to me, from where I sit, that the leaders of all your countries don't have a clue. They seem really disorganized, although your country, Dan, seems to be rolling out the vaccine pretty good. "Rolling out"—I just love the expressions you people come up with. In Toronto, Rod tells me, they don't seem to know what they're doing. All the politicians and medical people—I mean the medical bureaucrats, not the real doctors—keep saying that they have a plan and they're going to get needles in arms real quick. Another great expression— "needles in arms." You people crack me up.

And then there's a bunch of you people who think that COVID is some sort of a conspiracy, and that the vaccine is really a way for "them"—who knows who them is—to stick some sort of a computer chip into you people so you can be controlled. I love this story the best. No need for this, you're already controlled. You people invent all those norms and stuff and then you add laws, and then, when you break them, you're either deviant and get locked up, or you're radical and become a cultural studies professor. Some of you people even call yourselves anti-maskers and then say "we're fighting for freedom." This reminds me of a line in a song from a singer, Corin Raymond, who Rod and Tanya heard a few times; goes something like this—"sometimes you lower the bar and some-times the bar lowers you."[27] The bar of freedom is so low for these anti-maskers that they have to dig down into the ground a foot or so, just to walk over it.

I know that there's people in far more difficult situations than you, Dan, but this doesn't mean that your situation isn't difficult. That's the funny thing about situations—there's always people with worse ones and people with better ones. That's the situation.

You say that "my place, home—well, it feels like these walls are closing in." You feel "more confined" every day. "Days slip into nights," you say, "weekdays and weekends feel the same." All those everyday tasks, the ones you and so many of you people take for granted, the ones that felt so reassuring, tasks such as "morning coffee, regular walking routes," and lots more like these, have become "routinized," as you say. No wonder this COVID thing is a bit too much.

You know what's funny, Dan? Before COVID the everyday things you people did were also routinized and taken for granted. I know how much you hate this word, but these everyday things were normal. This is what makes you people take them for granted. Then, COVID comes along and disrupts, to use your word, the fuck out of normalcy! Normally, you disability studies people love to disrupt normalcy, at least you say you do. But I don't blame you people for this. The problem is that you want to disrupt on your own terms. Of course, I don't know where my preferred word, disturbance, comes in here. I guess if I were to be consistent, something else you people love, I'd have to say that COVID disturbs the peace, and this would mean it's an artist. Painted myself into a kennel, Dan—didn't I? COVID, an artist? No way!

Still, I don't blame you for getting down over this COVID thing. It's really disturbing and disrupting. You people do have to set up new routines and they're usually so different and so against the routines that COVID has ruined. What's most disruptive is that COVID seems to bring out the worst in you people, sometimes.

It reminds me a little of blindness. When I said that I tried to guide Rod out of his blind thing into a different, more creative blind thing, I think he was interpreting his blindness and feeling it in a similar way you people are now interpreting and feeling COVID. It's a bitch—again, I'm using this word the way you people do, but be careful, because one of these days we're gonna take that word back. Lots of you people see COVID and disability in much the same way—as a disturbance/disruption to life. Setting up new routines can be a real drag. Learning how to get around blind, talk to people blind, shop blind, shower, dress, eat meals, find the stuff you need in public bathrooms, the list goes on and on and on—finding new routines for blind is sometimes a real drag and very difficult. That might be the bad and the good of blindness, the ugly and the beautiful; it can be bad and ugly to set up new routines blind and can be even uglier to make them normal; it can be good and beautiful to have a "look"—don't tell Rod I used that word—at the world without all the routines and normal shit that are in it. That's got to be flat-out beautiful. Come to think of it, this is the blind thing I tried to guide Rod into, Dan.

I'm still laughing at how you called our disturbance/disruption debate a war. Nothing more disturbing or disrupting than that! That's a riot. I have to admit, we have something similar to wars. If there's something I want and some other dog wants it too, well—whoever seems the most scary—that's who gets it. Sometimes, I can just give the other dog a look and they back right off. Other times, a bit more than a look is called for. Come to think of it, Dan, maybe you people got the idea of war from us; but I think you people carried it a bit too far. Have another look at what we do and fix up this war thing you people have. You need us.

You say you never asked about my second name; but you did, remember? Just to remind you, I took a page out of your people's book; I'm—Smokie—just—Smokie. You have Pelé, Madonna, Cher, Prince, Coolio, Ruby, Rosa, and now—Smokie.

My disturbance might be your disruption and your disruption might be my disturbance, but I don't think they're different words with the same meaning or different meanings with the same word. It's not just semantics, like you say. Then again, I only ever had a small people vocabulary, and since I've been messing around up here with John it's gotten smaller. Don't tell Rod I said that either, Dan.

Okay, let's belabour it, Dan. You say that disruption has a more "external, extended, distributed feel to it than disturbance." You also want to keep disruption "because it has a less psychology-friendly vibe to it." I feel that whether you want to keep disturbance or not, it's going to hang around. And I think you're right; the two words might be similar, but they're also different. I like distinction better than difference, but maybe that's a war for another time. What you're saying is that disturbance is more psychological, a kind of feel, while disruption is more external to us, not so much a feel as a recognizable thing. I heard some of you people put this kind of thing this way—subjective versus objective—disturbance is subjective, disruption is objective. Is that what you mean? You people have so many ways of talking about stuff. Sometimes

I like it and sometimes I say—like I used to when Rod and I were together-together— "dude—you want to go left or right, stop with the 'I think' or the 'maybe'—which way?"

What I was trying to say before is that when we disrupt stuff, we put it back in some kind of order. We fix it. Another thing I was saying is that we can often disrupt stuff. Stuff can disrupt us too, but we can also do the disrupting. A traffic jam, for example, can disrupt you people; it never disrupted me when Rod and I were together-together, because I always found a way around it. Just thought I'd throw that in there. We can also protest and disrupt traffic, causing a traffic jam. We can disrupt on purpose.

Disturbance? I'm not sure. It seems to me something has to disturb. Funny thing is, the stuff that disturbs some people doesn't disturb others. It's subjective! I've come to learn—don't exactly know how I did but I did—about slavery. It didn't disrupt lots of people. But lots found it disturbing. Those people who found it disturbing started to disrupt it. Rod told me that Jill McConkey (I think she works for some sort of a press or something) was really interested in what I said about slavery. And she wrote an email to Rod saying, "Slavery disrupted whole ways of life for generations and millions found it disturbing for centuries before the few who had power to disrupt it were finally disturbed enough to disrupt it."[28] Now that's pretty good.

That was heavy. I'm gonna get a drink of water, Dan; I'll have to tell you about how I do that sometime. Be right back.

Okay, I'm ready; back to psychology. Lots of people look at psychology and are good with it, it doesn't disturb them. But it disturbs you. And, from what Rod and Tanya tell me, you're disrupting the fuck out of it. How the hell do you get along with all those educational psychologists you work with? Must be your good looks! You disrupt the fuck out of these educational psychologists and they still like you, you good-looking charmer you.

I'm not trying to convince you of anything. I'm just saying that I don't think disturbance and disruption can be so easily ripped apart by saying one is more internal or subjective, and the other more external or objective. You know what they are, Dan? It just came to me. I heard Rod making fun of this term, but you know him, he makes fun of everything. They're *relational.* Disturbance and disruption are related to one another, and if you have one without the other, then they lose their power.

You say that "disturbed people and disturbing minds are wanted as the very things on which psychologists can prey, and by extension, maintain their power." Sounds about right, Dan. But first, someone has to convince a whole bunch of you people that some of them and some of their minds can get disturbed. Someone also has to convince a whole bunch of you people how to recognize a disturbed mind when you come across it, even if it's your own. And then, more convincing is needed to make a bunch of you people think that these disturbed people and disturbed minds should and can be repaired. The final convincing—psychology can do this repairing because it's very powerful. Now, that's quite a logic to swallow. You say you "have a feeling that disruption is not as easily psychologized as disturbance." Again, Dan, not convinced. The media, especially the right-wing media, psychologized the fuck out of the Black Lives Matter protestors. They did the same thing during the Oka Crisis, Idle No More, Wet'suwet'en protests.[29] Here's a funny thing: I remember Rod telling me that some right-wing media in the States said that the BLM protestors were disturbed. There's that relationality thing again. I think you people can pretty much psychologize the hell out of anything. This seems to be a favourite pastime of you people. I remember not only doctors but also just people on the street psychologizing the hell out of that disturbing blindness of Rod's. Lots of you people, I remember, talked about Rod's blindness as too disrupting and that it would cause him all sorts of psychological problems. (Between you and me, Dan, blindness is the least of that dude's problems.)

Disturbance seems to still disturb you, Dan, especially, as you say, "when it is named, measured, or recognized, it's often in service of keeping the peace. The peace of normality." Whenever you people recognize anything, and then give it a name and on top of that measure it, all kinds of stuff can go wrong. I heard Rod and Tanya talking about what Thomas King said.[30] He's the Indigenous guy whose books I mentioned in another letter. He said something about Christianity, or Judeo-Christianity or something, and naming everything and then taking charge of everything! Can you believe it?! You people like to name everything you see. I'm pretty sure that when you people name something, you think it's yours. You even do that with us animals. You give us breeds and you even give us Latin names—how posh. All of this stuff is used to say what is normal and what isn't. I feel this has something to do with that eugenics thing you people talk about, you know, which people are better than other people, stuff like that.

I do get why you're a little scared of psychology. It does love to point to disturbance as something that went wrong with normalcy. That's scary. You say that psychology permits disturbance to "sit on the edges of the normal and is tolerated." Good point. Anything outside the norm is permitted to sit on the edges. Where else can it go? On the edge is a good place to put people that you people can't figure out what to do with. You people have put us animals and other people too on the edge since you got to walk on two legs. It seems to me that the edge is really a part of normalcy; no edge, no normalcy. And, no normalcy, no edge. That's what I find disturbing.

Disruption, you say, "feels more subversive, less easy to pin down, and reaches out to others in its practice of rupturing the taken-for-granted." Then you say that "disturbance is readily invited in by the status quo." It made me laugh when you said, "who really gets pissed off at a little disturbance?" I think you're right. You people might not get pissed off, but you sure get scared at even a little disturbance. No one gets scared of a little disruption.

You always give me lots to feel about, Dan. Sometimes, I feel that disruption, too, is tolerated by normalcy and invited in by the status quo. How else can normalcy turn itself into the "new normal"? You people love your new normals. I also feel that quite often when something is disrupted it just brings the full force of normalcy down on that disruption like a rockslide and crushes it and shapes it into a brand spanking new normal. I remember when Rod and I were together-together, his blindness would sometimes disrupt things. When he went into a classroom to teach sociology, I can remember, sometimes the whole place would act like—WTF! The fucking prof is blind!

How is he gonna teach us anything? And then, everything got normalized. Those students already knew what blindness was; they named it, measured it, and recognized it. After the initial shock, it didn't take too long for Rod to be recognized as someone who would do things differently. What did hang around, though, was Rod's blindness, and for so many of those students, and a bunch of the professors too, this was disturbing and remained so. It seemed like disruption could fit right into the status quo as new normal or difference—but disturbance . . . different story.

I was telling you once, Dan, about how I hear a lot of Rod and Tanya's academic friends talking in this funny way, using this funny language. They say things like "neoliberal" or "late capitalism" or "individualism," stuff like that. Now, a feeling that came to me one day when I was contemplating the stuff you were saying about disturbance and disruption is that if this stuff is true, I mean, this neoliberal stuff, then you people need psychology. It seems to me that that's the only sense of what it means to be human that neoliberalism and capitalism will tolerate. How are you people going to disrupt this neoliberal thing? I hear that even after the BLM movement, a bunch of Americans, including those right-wing politicians, still think there's no racism! The commissioner of the Royal Canadian Mounted Police in Canada thinks that there's no systemic racism in the RCMP! Rod and Tanya just told me of a report that came out of your country that said a murder of a Black kid about eighteen years ago had nothing to do with racism! This is the twenty-first century! What the hell did all the disruption disrupt? Seems like disruption usually makes the thing disrupted get stronger.

This COVID-19 thing has disrupted the fuck out of everything. If things are gonna change, I feel that disruption needs to be blended up a little bit with some disturbance. You people should be disturbed at just how weak and fragile you are. This COVID-19 pandemic should be disturbing the hell out of you people and it should be making you a little more humble in the face of all life, including what you people call non-human life. It comes down to—

You need us.

But, like you say, "disturbance seems to really have been owned by psychology." Maybe you're right, Dan, maybe disturbance can't be reclaimed. I know one thing, though—psychology doesn't have to own us or you people. Here's a little hope: "crip" has been reclaimed, at least a little, and so has the "N-word" and "NDN." Watch out 'cause we dogs are going to reclaim "bitch." And if you people add a little disruption to this mix—who knows?—maybe revolution.

It seems to me that psychology owns many of you people because you've sold yourselves out to neoliberalism and its sidekick psychology. Can't have one without the other. That neoliberal guy needs the individual. Here's something funny: psychology is like a neoliberal's guide; it's like a really poorly trained guide dog leading neoliberalism all over the place. You people need a new guide dog for neoliberalism so that it can lead it on the right path, right out of itself.

You say that disturbance is so controlled and monitored by psychology that it may have lost its "radical purchase in the world." Didn't the same thing happen to disability studies? Isn't it controlled and monitored by psychology? Doesn't psychology even control and monitor what counts as a disability, all disabilities—physical, visible, invisible, cognitive—everything? You people need a breakup; break up with psychology. It's gonna ask for a lot of alimony; but don't pay it. Stick to what you people, the human, need. It's high time you people thought of "need" as something other than psychological. Come to think of it, it's also time you people thought of accessibility as something other than fitting people like Rod into the world. All psychology wants is a new normal. Break up, Dan—now. This advice—it's coming from me and John. Tell us what you want to revolutionize, and John and I can tell you whether you can count us in or count us out.

I can't help getting the feeling that you want to be out of psychology very badly. But you can't seem to break up with it. It's as though you need something to lead you out—disruption. You don't want to consider psychology your "home," and yet you need a disruption to lead you out; I wonder if you might mean that you don't want to consider psychology your home *anymore* and that you are having trouble getting out and that's why you need disruption. That's fair enough. Psychology seems to be your academic home, and it's not a very good one. I get it. Time to leave home.

You want your new home to be "the school and the street." In the schools and in the streets, we can experience, as you say, kids disrupting classrooms, Black lives disrupting white supremacy, blindness disrupting sight, and Indigenous lives and disability disrupting everything (you didn't say this last thing, I threw it in, just to remind you). This will give us, you say, a "together-togetherness that disrupts the isolating consequences associated with the usual tales of blindness and disability." You're right, Dan, this is disruption. The fear I have comes from something I've noticed about you people and disruption. Every time something gets disrupted, it seems temporary. Normalcy is involved here, and I think that normalcy has yet to be thought about by you people, especially those of you who say you do disability studies. What Rod and I did together-together was anything but normal. You stick someone like me, a dog, into a harness; you teach me a whole bunch of people words; and you teach me to act quite human in non-dog places. Now that takes a postgraduate education. There's nothing normal either about one of you people doing exactly what a dog tells you to. If this doesn't disrupt the norm of person and dog together, then I don't know what does. But it didn't take too long of Rod and me being together-together (and not just together) for *our* together-togetherness to feel very normal; it's just who we were, and maybe still are.

And my fear goes beyond this, like I said before. Disruption is temporary because you people adjust and create what you are now calling a "new normal." This normalcy thing, I feel, is way more powerful and flexible than you people seem to think. It's true what you say about disturbance being psychologized and something that psychology loves, but psychology has the same relationship with adjustment. You people adjust; that's the thing you do. No matter what the disturbance, you people adjust. Quite often, you people find it very difficult to adjust, but you keep trying. Take this COVID-19. It's disruptive AF and, difficult as it is, you people keep on adjusting. You even psychologized your adjustment; you people say things like "COVID fatigue"; I even heard someone say "COVID head." I feel, Dan, that psychology loves both disturbance and disruption.

Disruption often feels more exciting than disturbance, as you say. You think that maybe the excitement you feel about disruption is a symptom of COVID-19. You think it might even be a "reaching out for something that feels like a radical break with the everyday." It made me laugh, Dan, when you said that this might be "the pains of living life as a recovering psychologist." You're right.

One thing I do feel is that disturbance/disruption is not a semantic or a tomato/tomahto thing or anything like that. I think disruption and disturbance are different even though they're related, maybe even closely related. Another thing I feel (know) for sure is that disruption doesn't disrupt the peace of normalcy. It may ruffle its feathers (I love that human expression), but the peace of normalcy will return, sooner or later.

It seems to me that what's needed is to experience that peace of normalcy as disturbing. This might be what you call a radical shift from the everyday. The everyday can get very peaceful. I even hear you people say things like "I'm in a rut"—then you people say you have to change things. You people take some of this everyday, stick it into a little piece of a new everyday, and—voila—a new normal. The taken-for-granted will always be; the everyday will always be; what doesn't need to always be is to take the taken-for-granted for granted. Every now and then, you people can disturb the peace that it brings and this brings the realization that the taken-for-granted, the everyday, is not your home, the foundation of your life, but only a way to establish some common ground for all differences and distinctions to be together. The problem is that you people focus on difference rather than distinction, and then, if that's not enough, put these differences into some kind of a hierarchy making all kinds of shit. That's what you people do. You people are going to have to find a way to understand difference, distinction, and especially normalcy. You take these things for granted, especially in activities such as DS, and this is one of the reasons disruption is so exciting. It's always exciting to move the pieces of difference around—putting the bottom piece on the top and the top piece on the bottom. The pieces, though, remain. Nothing disturbed, merely disrupted.

I think you're right, Dan; what brings us together is our sense of unease with the taken-for-granted and how it just keeps rolling on by. I don't think that it's "untouched by others," as you say. It is the touch of everyone that created this taken-for-granted and it is the gentle touch of everyone that keeps it "rolling on by." I feel that it is this "touch" that needs exploration. Here's a question: How would you disrupt this touch?

As you say, there are "zones of peaceful tranquillity," of regular ways of experiencing life, of the peaceful feel of the status quo, and, "any entity that disturbs or disrupts the peace is always rendered undesirable." You did it again—you provided me with some words, some "people" words that really help me to say what I want to. If something disturbs or disrupts, it's undesirable—you people just don't want it. We're pretty much the same. We (animals) put our worlds together largely through feel, what you people call instinct; through routine, what you people call training; and through taken-for-granted sets of expectations, what you people call norms. When this stuff works without a hitch, we sometimes find it to be peaceful. It's a kind of peace that allows us to move through our lives without much thought, without really thinking about this life-movement. Our life-movement, of course, is influenced and shaped by all kinds of shit—needs, desires, loves, hates, aspirations—and all this shit is shaped by who gets to say what's real and what's normal (you people sometimes call this power). How a movement gets defined as a life-movement—and which of these movements get defined as desirable, undesirable, normal, abnormal, and all the other definitions you people are so fond of—this is what you people need to consider.

Here's the thing your words helped me say, Dan: It seems to me that the most disturbing and disruptive thing you people can do is to think about and get a feel for what sort of peace we (all of us) need in order for our life together to be transformed into togetherness, a life together-together. Don't know if I said that well enough, Dan, but that's what I feel a together-together peace might be.

The other thing you made me feel with your words about how Rod and I moved in the world together-together, in our life-movement, as you put it, in our "journeys, routes, destinations," is that peace must be located somewhere in these routes and destinations, in our life-movements. Finding new routes could lead to new destinations; travelling the same routes in different ways may lead us to the same destinations experienced in different ways. I'm no decolonizer of space, as you suggest, Dan. I just loved moving; movement was and still is my love; togetherness seems to be the only way to move and my together-together time with Rod was a life-movement that I continually relive, and I feel (know) that Rod does too.

I found this thing you said, "shared animality/humanity" disruptive and disturbing; I don't know whether I gave us a new way of thinking about our interconnections and a new route into them, just wanted to let you know how I felt about our life together, our animal/human life together. Most important, I wanted to let you know just how much you and the three Rs—that's what Rod sometimes calls Rebecca, Ruby, and Rosa—mean to him. I wanted you to know, too, how much Rod loves you and appreciates everything you do and say. And I have a feeling that when you are with Rod, you're together-together and that somehow you picked up the activity of guiding him into a blindness that the world you people created for yourselves hasn't even glimpsed.

The word "journey" is overused as much here as it is in the UK. There's as many reality shows here as in the UK as well. And "those people" who are on these reality shows and who watch them think that they're on some kind of journey and, like you say, they don't want the journey to end. Lots of you people here in Canada think the same way about their lives. Rod and I were at someone's retirement a number of years ago, and I remember the guy who was retiring saying something like, "This has been a great journey, now it's coming to an end and I'm embarking on a new journey." Unbelievable! There are also some of you people who keep a journal about your journeys. It never ends. But what if we feel that journey is a life-movement? Where would this get us? And, what if we felt (thought) of life-movement as a movement into change, personal and together, individual and collective, as you people put it? This would mean that any life-movement without change wouldn't be worth the journey. And any change, personal or collective, without the pains of growth isn't worth the journey either. New routes, travelling old routes in differ-ent ways, new destinations, visiting old destinations in different ways—this has to lead to some kind of revolutionary change. Guiding Rod through strange and familiar routes of blindness, arriving at strange and familiar destinations, deciding to live in the movement of a strange familiarity with one another, with blindness and with the world—this together-together way of life is something I wish, I truly do, that everyone (all of us) could experience . . . even if for a little while.

The Town Called Malice—as strange as you and The Jam make this town out to be, Rod and I travelled its streets many times. We had a blast doing so. Rod and I let them know, in the way we moved, that blindness was ours, not theirs. This made them angry—mostly at Rod; I was in the clear. At times like this, I played the "dumb dog," Dan, I really did. When we left the streets of the Town Called Malice, Rod would say— "Thanks, Smoke; glad you were there for me." I would just laugh and say, "no problem," and continue taking Rod into a blindness neither he nor I knew, but a blindness both of us were quite excited to "see"—again Dan, don't tell Rod I used that word. Like you, Dan, I have no idea what sort of disturbance or disruption will "shatter the status quo" of blindness found in the Town Called Malice. I think you might be right, this Town Called Malice may be "beyond saving," and you also might be right that "journeying to this part of the world will only end in tears."

I couldn't agree with you more, Dan—Rod and I did travel a different route of blindness and we did end up in a much different place from the Town Called Malice. And I am chuffed (Rod taught me this word) that you gave the name Nottingham to this new town of blindness, the streets of which Rod and I travelled together-together. I humbly accept

Nottingham as the name for blindness that Rod and I created as we moved, and I am more than humbled to follow in the tracks of Nottingham's most famous son—you.

We may have missed a point in our disturbance/disruption debate. Even so, the point is, from what I can tell, that you and I really want—it's like a visceral need for us—to disturb and disrupt. I have a feeling, since that's mostly all I have, that you and I, rather than disturbing and disrupting, may just be disturbance and disruption. Maybe others have to make something of this; maybe this is another form of together-together. Maybe we do need to take new roads and routes and get to new destinations and stay there a while . . . or longer. From what Rod tells me and from what Tanya tells me, too, the roads and routes that the six of you—they, you, Rebecca, Rosa, and Ruby—follow lead you to destinations never before experienced by by the six of you. You seem to make old routes new, old destinations new, and new routes and new destinations feel so at home that it seems that you've travelled them and been there before. I'm envious, Dan. You're not supposed to feel stuff like envy where I am, so don't say anything.

The train journey you had with the learning disabled people sounds like, to me, one of those beautifully disturbing and disruptive times. The people on the train did lead you to another place, another home of learning disability; but, don't forget, Dan, you got them on the train.

Home—you're right, Dan, that's a good name for the place of blindness Rod and I travelled in and a good name for the place of learning disability the people on the train took you to. Rod and I were "going home" and we were "on our way home"—I was guiding Rod into the home of blindness and, the weird thing, Dan, I felt at home there, too.

One little danger; don't let those "professionals," even if they go by the name "staff," turn learning disabled people into "experts" about themselves. That doesn't disrupt or disturb any notion of expertise where someone like Rod is someone from whom expertise can be gleaned. An alternative is to get learning disabled people and Rod to become experts on the experts. It's those experts who need to be studied, not learning disabled and blind people.

By the way, are you sure John didn't write that song? Are you sure it was Paul? John and Paul—alone-together, together-together—in Abbey Road, just the two of them, recording that beautiful song; an acoustic guitar and a bass and, as you point out, sheer joy. I remember that joy and here comes another tear I'll paw away. One human, one dog—alone-together, together-together—Rod and Smokie, Smokie and Rod; one pair of sneakers, one guide dog harness—sheer joy. Here comes another tear, Dan.

Rod tells me he feels the same as you do—unsettled, agitated, impatient, and, of course, distracted. This COVID-19 thing has done a number on you people. You people have been asked to isolate, stay at home, lock down, and all those other funny ways you people have of expressing yourselves. The only time I ever felt like that was when I was in residence at postgraduate school—they called it the "kennel." Like you, I wanted outta Dodge and Rod was my way out. I tried my best to guide Rod to the place you mentioned, Dan—to a place where blindness isn't "already known," but instead to a place where blindness is "imagined together on a journey."

We (non-humans) do this kind of shit all the time; imagine, I mean. (And you wonder why John and I get on together so well.) I got outta Dodge with Rod, outta that postgraduate residence, and, I felt, Let's find a blindness that's way less restricting than the one they taught me about in postgraduate school. Let's imagine blindness as a journey, I said to Rod, and let's—boogie! And, you know Dan, we did, for so many years (especially my type of years); we did.

I think you're right, Dan, blindness is a commingling of tales of travel, people, and locations. Never fear, Dan, our journey, our travels, will never end. I didn't have it in my feel, in my mind, but now that you mention it, I feel that's what art must be, as you say, "to be more than alive." I'm going to mention that to John; betcha a tenner he writes a song, a follow-up to "Imagine."

"The chance to travel and imagine together" is the most precious gift we can give to one another, as you say, Dan. I've been travelling with you (together-together) through all these letters, and truth be known, for a longer time than that. No matter where Rod and Tanya go, where they travel, they go and travel with you and the three Rs. And the places and times the six of you have travelled together-together are the places and times Rod and Tanya recount to others here in Toronto. Our journey never ends, Dan, because our imaginations never do.

Well, well, Dan, the final letter. I think it's a good idea to end this first series of letters between us. I said first series because I think there will be more things to talk about. Even though we never met in the flesh, we got to know each other quite well, as you say, and it seems like we have a lot more to talk about. So, you never know.

I had one more thing I wanted to tell you, but I really couldn't find the right time so far; so, I thought I'd leave it to the end. It's nothing that I want you to respond to necessarily, Dan, it's just something I want to tell you; something I want to get off my chest, as you people say. So, bear with me.

You know how I always use the term together-together when I'm talking to you about those times Rod and I, Tanya, and the rest of them lived in Toronto and then in Antigonish and how I don't use together-together to talk about Rod and me being together now. Well, I was thinking about what you said in one of your letters and that maybe Rod and I are still together-together, even now. Maybe that's true, Dan. Our togetherness feels a little different now than it did before, but maybe you're right and this feel of different togetherness doesn't mean we're not together-together.

The point is, I really miss how Rod and I were together-together. You know how I said that I sometimes have to paw a tear away when I feel those times—well, it's more than sometimes—it's lots of times. And the other thing is that I know Rod feels the same way and he rubs tears away lots of times, too.

We're still together, maybe even together-together. We are talking, what you people call communicating, all the time. We're reminiscing, he's telling me about all kinds of stuff he's been writing, he tells me about all the different people he and Tanya have met and become friends with, and he tells me about you and the three Rs—a lot. So, we're in touch. We have never been out of touch, not since I met him at the guide dog training school.

About—I'm not exactly sure how long ago in your people's years—but, I'm guessing about two or three years ago, I decided to do something to get Rod and me a little more together, maybe together-together. So, here's the part I wanted to tell you, Dan: I started to come to him in dreams. I already mentioned this. It really is a secret. I'll tell you anyways, so here goes. Of course, I always did come to him in dreams; he dreamt of me, I dreamt of him, ever since we knew each other. But I decided to come to him in dreams more often—about two or three times a week.

I'm not sure that was such a good idea; that's the thing I wanted to tell you, Dan. I love meeting up with Rod in dreams and doing some of the stuff we used to do, I really love it. But it sometimes gets Rod quite upset; not angry or anything like that, just what you people call emotional. Sometimes, he even has a rough day after we meet up in dreams, missing me, it seems, even more. The other thing he does sometimes is to make one of our dreams a real rough one. We'll meet up in the dream—maybe we're playing in a park, maybe walking down Yonge Street—and then Rod dreams that something bad happens to me—I hurt my paw or I get lost and he can't find me, something like that. And then the next couple of days are really rough for him.

I don't know why he does that. What I've been feeling about it, and it's just a feeling, is that he feels really badly that I'm not around anymore and he sometimes feels even worse when he thinks about some of the disagreements we had, like those times we walked by an aggressive dog and I got pissed off. He let me know not to do shit like that. I feel that, when he remembers things like that, he feels badly. Maybe that's why he brings stuff into our dreams where I'm getting hurt or lost or something.

I considered what you said about Rod and me still being together-together—I even talked about it with John—and you're right; Rod and I are still together-together. So, what I decided to do is what I did when we were first together-together—I'm gonna guide him through our dreams—together-together. I'm not going to stop coming to Rod in dreams and I'm not going to do it less often either.

I can't thank you enough, Dan. We spoke a lot over the last few months and got to know each other very well. That was definitely a beautiful gift. But this gift—this gift you gave me, Dan—it brought a tear to my eye. You made me a guide dog again, Dan.

Just so you know, Dan, I've been talking to George, too, and even he says John was the best Beatle. Go big Red Machine.[31] Loads of love from the good place.

Your friend forever,
Smokie

Afterword

Smoke!

It's been too, too long.

I bet you were thinking, Typical human, gets what he needs from the working dog, secures the book manuscript contract, and then fucks off into the ether.

I apologize for my tardiness. What can I say? I'm very important and busy!

I wanted to say thank you—from my heart—for guiding me through the lockdown. Rereading our letters I was reminded just how much you gave to me; how necessary your thoughts, reflections, humour, and challenges were to me during an awful, awful time.

Rod has probably told you, but we got the reviews back on *Letters with Smokie*. I won't dignify some of the "critical" comments by repeating them, but it turns out that some humans, well, they just don't get it, do they? They need a lot more animalization in their lives, that's for sure. Two reviewers did get it—and I think they've probably been in touch with you in some way or another to share their appreciation.

At last Rod and Tanya are back in the UK this week.

We will raise more than one glass to you, Smokie.

"We all made it through the pandemic," we'll shout, "and we couldn't have done it without Smokie—Cheers."

Thanks, Smokie, truly. You are always with us.
Love ya,
Your friend and brother,
Dan x

Afterword

Hi Dan,

Let me say, Dan, when Rod told me this morning that I had a letter from you, well, I was thrilled! No need to apologize for not writing. Those letters we shared over those horrible months of lockdown you people were having was something I enjoyed just as much as you did. I could have written you just as easily as you could have written me. So, like I said, no need for apologies.

I'm really happy that you and Rod got a book out of those letters. Like I said to Rod when he told me about the book contract last week, "You're welcome." Just kidding. I think you're right; many of your people need to pay more attention to us animals. I've noticed that humans can get quite self-im-portant if there isn't anything in their lives that can make them a little humble. Sometimes animals can do that. Some of us will do stuff for you people and love you people without any conditions whatsoever and this can often be humbling. Imagine being able to do something just for the love of it or imagine loving someone just for loving them. So often there seem to be strings attached to these sorts of things for you people; but that's something for a later discussion.

For now, I want to tell you how much I appreciated exchang-ing letters with you during the pandemic, Dan. It was incredible! It gave me a chance to reflect on my life together-together with Rod and how we moved in the world in that blind thing. It also gave me a chance to think about my guiding and about me as a guide. A guide—me; sometimes I have trouble thinking that.

Our letters, Dan: what an experience. We talked about more things in those letters than most of you people do in a lifetime. I'm not talking about you professors. You're always talking about stuff like this. I'm talking about people who think they know everything about everything, and don't need to think about anything anymore. Wait a minute. Maybe I am talking about professors. Just kidding.

The other thing is that I get to write a book about my life together-together with Rod. He wrote *The Two in One* and I didn't get a chance to say anything in that one. Now, it's my turn; these letters with you let me talk about a lot of stuff, especially about what Rod had to say in *The Two in One*. These letters were a real blast. And now—a book!

I'm the one who should be thanking you, Dan. You gave me a chance to think about stuff and to talk about them with you. More than anything else, I got to know you. This means so much to me.

I am so happy that Rod and Tanya are headed to the UK. They love it there with you and the rest of your family and they love Manchester. They're quite excited. The only trouble, Dan, is that Rod will be speaking a lot of British when he gets back. But he and Tanya will be re-energized by spending time with all of you, and this makes me happy.

Well, let's hope this book sells. Think they'll make a movie out of it? Who's going to play us, Dan?

A whole bunch of love from your friend and brother.
Smokie

P.S. I'm thinkin' that maybe I might come to you in dreams, too.

Acknowledgements

It's not often that a dog writes a book. I'd like to thank Dan and Rod for helping me out with this magnum opus! Any mistakes are theirs alone. There's a number of humans that Rod, Dan, and I would like to thank. Thanks to Maddy De Welles for typing all of Rod's mumblings on his new digital Dictaphone. He thinks it is still not as good as his old micro-cassette tape one. I owe thanks to Nate Bitton for going over earlier drafts of my book with Rod. Thanks to Deb Goodley, Dan's mom, for offering really helpful written feedback in the early drafts. Much gratitude, too, to Efrat Gold for editing this text with aplomb and a pen. I am grateful to Elaine Cagulada for proof-reading the page proofs. I am especially grateful to Tanya Titchkosky for not only sharing her life with me but also for the love she showed and continues to show for all animals and their place in this world. Much love to you, Tanya. Even though everyone says you have a poor memory, I think it's incredible how well you remember our life together-together. Thanks to the following people who continue to support Rod and Dan through life: Rebecca Lawthom, Rosa Cariad Lawthom Goodley, Ruby Haf Lawthom Goodley, Alan Goodley, Heather

Berkeley, Radek Puky, Brian Clough, Devon Healey, Dan Ahern, and his late wife, Annette, and their two sons Brendan and Aidan, as well as Dan and Judy MacInnes and their kids. Rod and Dan are grateful to the anonymous reviewers for their comments on this book. They owe a great deal of thanks to Jill McConkey of the University of Manitoba Press; she showed great interest in my book and guided it through the publishing process. I am especially indebted to the guide dogs that graduated with me: Colonel, Megan, Sheba, and Jonesy. I am also grateful to the friendship of Sparky, Homer, and Kuma, and their people Celia, Dave, and Isabel. Finally, my love goes out to my sisters Cassis, Jessie, and Sugar.

Smokie
May 2023

Notes

INTRODUCTION

1 Michalko, *The Two in One*, 57–58.

2 Dan is referring here to the FAO, OIE, WHO 2010's pithily entitled report, "FAO–OIE–WHO Collaboration: Sharing Responsibilities and Coordinating Global Activities to Address Health Risks at the Animal–Human–Ecosystems Interfaces: A Tripartite Concept Note."

3 This is a direct quote from Hayles's 2021 thought-provoking paper entitled "Fearing the Wrong Boogeyman: COVID Vaccines."

THE LETTERS

1 I am referring to Dan's *Disability and Other Human Questions*.

2 This refers to an encounter Smokie and I had with a stranger on a street in Toronto one day, where the stranger asked me if my dog was a "blind dog." "I hope not," I had replied. I tell this story in detail in my book *The Two in One*, 41–51.

3 "The three of them"—refers to Cassis (Tanya's little black lab) and Jessie and Sugar (our two cats). Like Smokie, they too have passed.

4 Dan is referring to the 2009 conference of the Society for Disability Studies in Tucson, Arizona.

5 This is from Rosi Braidotti's *The Posthuman*, in which the author furthers an analysis of humankind that critically explores a number of deep human and non-human connections and tensions.

6   See the wonderful Sunaura Taylor's *Beasts of Burden*. Taylor offers a very persuasive and sensitive take on the intimate relations between animals and disabled human beings.

7   Smokie is probably speaking here of a conversation he heard between me and a PhD student where I spoke of the body as something humans are rather than as a thing that humans have. I made reference to an edited collection that I have used in one of my courses: Fraser and Greco, *The Body*.

8   Dan is thinking here of the seminal text by Oliver, *The Politics of Disablement*. Oliver was the first professor of disability studies in the UK and has been recognized as one of the first proponents of the social model of disability, an understanding of disability developed by the British disabled people's movement that seeks to identify and challenge the exclusionary—or disabling—ways in which society responds to the phenomenon of impairment.

9   Dan is referring to a well-rehearsed argument of the social model of disability, in which we are encouraged to interrogate the social pathologies of discrimination and exclusion that render people with impairments as less than human. See Morris, *Pride against Prejudice*—a wonderful text for accessing further analysis.

10 Smokie is likely referring here to my reference to Heidegger, *What Is Called Thinking*, where he writes "*Most thought-provoking is that we are still not thinking . . .*" (p. 4, italics in original).

11 This refers to Thomas King's children's books, probably *A Coyote Columbus Story; A Coyote Solstice Tale;* and *Coyote Tales*. Tanya and I have read these books together: Tanya reading aloud, of course. Years later, Tanya actually used *A Coyote Columbus Story* as a reading in one of her graduate classes. If you're interested in Indigenous understandings of human/non-human animal relations check out the work of Zoe Todd and Daniel Heath Justice.

12 The social model of disability posits a shift in focus from disability as biological deficit (the notion that impairment equates with disability) to disability as a societal deficit (the idea that people with impairments are excluded by society). See, for instance, Oliver, *Politics of Disablement*; Oliver, "Understanding Disability"; Shakespeare, *Disability Studies Reader*.

13 Eve Haque is a professor of sociolinguistics at York University, Toronto, and a friend of Rod's and Tanya's. She has said that the city's slogan should be "Toronto—the broken city that hates its people."

14 Dan is referring to Titchkosky, *The Question of Access*. Access is a huge problem for many disabled people in a society that is simply not geared

up for disabled people; but Tanya also considers access as an opportunity to interrogate the ways in which some of us are permitted to be included while others are forced to occupy more peripheral positions in the world.

15 Baldwin, "The Creative Process."

16 Beatles, "Revolution 1," by John Lennon and Paul McCartney, on *The Beatles*, 1968.

17 Dan is thinking with writers who have challenged the practices of psychologization. See, for instance, De Vos, *Psychologisation in Times of Globalisation*.

18 Dan is referring to a new research project entitled Humanising the Healthcare of People with Learning Disabilities (including people who also have autism). More details can be found at https://sites.google.com/sheffield.ac.uk/esrchumanisinghealthcare/home.

19 It is difficult for me to say exactly where Smokie heard this. When he says that "some people say that blindness disrupts sight," he is likely referring to the many times he's heard me say something like this in classrooms or in discussions with people, and to how I criticize the idea that blindness automatically disrupts sight.

20 Smokie is taking liberty with the words of David Mitchell, words that he heard me say at some point. Mitchell writes, "Nearly every culture views disability as a problem in need of a solution." Mitchell, "Narrative Prosthesis and the Materiality of Metaphor," 15.

21 Kris Kristofferson, "The Pilgrim: Chapter 33," on *The Silver Tounged Devil and I*, 1971.

22 Dan is referring to a high-profile Toronto debate in 2019 between Jordan Peterson and Slavoj Žižek (https://www.youtube.com/watch?v=lsWndf-zuOc4). In truth, the event was more of a love-in than a proper debate.

23 *Crip Camp: A Disability Revolution*, directed by Nicole Newnham and Jim LeBrecht, 2020, on Netflix, https://www.netflix.com/gb/title/81001496.

24 People First groups are self-advocacy groups, collectives run by and for people with intellectual disabilities. The People First movement is now an international assemblage fighting for the rights and recognition of people so-labelled, and these groups can be found all over the world using the motto, "Label Jars Not People" (www.peoplefirst.org; in Canada, www.peoplefirstofcanada.ca).

25 This is an excerpt from Goodley, *Disability and Other Human Questions*, Dan's book that prompted the first letter of congratulations from Smokie.

26 Beatles, "Two of Us," by John Lennon and Paul McCartney, on *Let it Be*, 1970.

27 Corin Raymond, "Some Nights the Bar Lowers You," on *Dirty Mansions*, 2019.

28 This sentence comes from Jill McConkey, acquisitions editor for the University of Manitoba Press. Smokie, impressed with how Jill listened to what he was saying, asked if he could just use it because it helped him say what he meant. Jill gave her permission.

29 Smokie is referring here to what he heard me talking about with someone (likely Tanya) regarding Indigenous peoples' protests and movements in Canada. Consider, for example, Palmater, *Warrior Life*; Obomsawin, *Kanehsatake*; the Kino-nda-niimi Collective, *The Winter We Danced*; McIvor, "Reconciliation on Trial."

30 Smokie seems to be recalling a conversation that Tanya and I had with respect to King's book of essays *The Truth about Stories*, particularly the introduction.

31 Smokie is referring here to the football club Nottingham Forest Football Club, Dan's favourite. Dan says, "Their 'kit' (as we say in the UK to refer to their uniform/colours) is red." Nottingham Forest won back-to-back European Cups in 1979 and 1980. They finally got promoted back to the Premiership in summer 2022. Forest's most famous manager was a man called Brian Clough. During the last few years of his time as manager, Clough would be accompanied to training sessions by his Golden Labrador, Del-Boy. There is yet to be a book capturing Del-Boy's no doubt illuminating stories of Clough's triumphs.

Bibliography

Ahmed, Sara. *Queer Phenomenology: Orientations, Objects, Others*. Durham, NC: Duke University Press, 2006.

Alcoff, Linda. "What Should White People Do?" *Hypatia* 13, no. 3 (1998): 6–26.

Al-Saji, Alia. "A Phenomenology of Hesitation: Interrupting Racialized Habits of Seeing." In *Living Alterities: Phenomenology, Embodiment, and Race*, edited by Emily Lee, 133–72. New York: State University of New York Press, 2014.

Arluke, Arnold, and Clinton Sanders. *Regarding Animals*. Philadelphia: Temple University Press, 1996.

Baldwin, James. "The Creative Process." In *Creative America*, edited by John F. Kennedy, Dwight D. Eisenhower, Harry S. Truman, et al. New York: The Ridge Press, 1962. Available at *AGITATE!* https://Agitatejournal. org/The-Creative-Process.

Bell, Christopher M. *Blackness and Disability: Critical Examinations and Cultural Interventions*. East Lansing: Michigan State University Press, 2011.

Braidotti, Rosi. *The Posthuman*. London: Polity Press, 2013.

Brim, Matt. *James Baldwin and the Queer Imagination*. Ann Arbor: University of Michigan Press, 2014.

De Vos, Jan. *Psychologisation in Times of Globalization*. London: Routledge, 2012.

Dubois, W.E.B. *The Souls of Black Folk*. New York: Penguin, 1903.

Erevelles, Nirmala, and Andrea Minear. "Unspeakable Offenses: Untangling Race and Disability in Discourses of Intersectionality." *Journal of Literary and Cultural Disability Studies* 4, no. 2 (2010): 127–45.

Fanon, Frantz. *Black Skin, White Masks.* New York: Grove Press, 1967.

"FAO–OIE–WHO Collaboration: Sharing Responsibilities and Coordinating Global Activities to Address Health Risks at the Animal–Human–Ecosystems Interfaces: A Tripartite Concept Note." Food and Agriculture Organization of the United Nations. April 2010. https://www.fao.org/3/ak736e/ak736e00.pdf.

Fraser, Mariam, and Monica Greco, eds. *The Body: A Reader.* London: Routledge, 2005.

Garland-Thomson, Rosemarie. "The Politics of Staring: Visual Rhetorics of Disability in Popular Photography." In *Disability Studies: Enabling the Humanities,* edited by Sharon L. Snyder, Brenda Jo Brueggemann, and Rosemarie Garland-Thomson, 56–75. New York: Modern Languages Association of America, 2002.

———. "Integrating Disability, Transforming Feminist Theory." *NWSA Journal* 14, no. 3 (Autumn 2002): 1–32.

Goffman, Erving. *Stigma: Notes on the Management of Spoiled Identity.* New Jersey: Prentice Hall, 1963.

Goodley, Dan. *Disability and Other Human Questions.* London: Emerald Publishing Ltd., 2020.

———. *Disability Studies: An Inter-Disciplinary Introduction.* 2nd ed. London: Sage, 2016.

———. *Dis/ability Studies: Theorising Disablism and Ableism.* London: Routledge, 2014.

Gordon, Lewis R. *Fear of Black Consciousness.* New York: Farrar, Straus and Giroux, 2022.

Hall, Kim Q. "No Failure: Climate Change, Radical Hope, and Queer Crip Feminist Eco-Future." *Radical Philosophy Review* 17, no. 1 (2014): 203–25.

Haraway, Donna Jeanne. *Primate Visions: Gender, Race and Nature in the World of Modern Science.* New York: Routledge, 1989.

Haque, Eve. *Multiculturalism within a Bilingual Framework: Language, Race, and Belonging in Canada.* Toronto: University of Toronto Press, 2012.

Hayles, Katherine. "Fearing the Wrong Boogeyman: COVID Vaccines." Online paper, February 2021. https://nkhayles.com/articles/ (accessed 29 April 2021).

———. *How We Became Posthuman: Virtual Bodies in Cybernetics, Literature, and Informatics.* Chicago: University of Chicago Press, 1999.

Healey, Devon. *Dramatizing Blindness: Disability Studies as Critical Creative Narrative*. London: Palgrave Macmillan, 2021.

Heidegger, Martin. *What Is Called Thinking?* Trans. Fred D. Wieck and J. Glenn Gray. New York: Harper and Row Publishers, 1968.

Hughes, Bill, and Kevin Patterson. "The Social Model of Disability and the Disappearing Body: Toward a Sociology of Impairment." *Disability and Society* 12, no. 3 (1997): 325–40.

Hunt, Paul. *Stigma: The Experience of Disability*. London: Geoffrey Chapman, 1966.

Jay, Martin. *Downcast Eyes: The Denigration of Vison in Twentieth-Century French Thought*. Berkeley: University of California Press, 1993.

Justice, Daniel Heath. *Badger*. Chicago: University of Chicago Press, 2015.

———. *Racoon*. Chicago: University of Chicago Press, 2021.

King, Thomas. *A Coyote Columbus Story*. Toronto: Groundwood Books, 1992.

———. *A Coyote Solstice Tale*. Toronto: Groundwood Books, 2009.

———. *Coyote Tales*. Groundwood Books, 2017.

———. *Green Grass, Running Water*. Toronto: Harper Perennial Canada, 1999.

———. *The Inconvenient Indian: A Curious Account of Native People in North America*. Toronto: Anchor Canada, 2012.

———. *The Truth about Stories*. Toronto: House of Anansi Press, 2003.

The Kino-nda-niimi Collective. *The Winter We Danced: Voices from the Past, the Future, and the Idle No More Movement*. Winnipeg: Arbeiter Ring Publishing, 2014.

Linton, Simi. *Claiming Disability: Knowledge and Identity*. New York: NYU Press, 1998.

Manning, Dolleen Tisawii'ashii. "The Murmuration of Birds: An Anishinaabe Ontology of Mnidoo-Worlding." In *Feminist Phenomenology Futures*, edited by Helen A. Fielding and Dorothea E. Olkowski, 154–82. Bloomington: Indiana University Press, 2017.

McIvor, Bruce. "Reconciliation on Trial: Wet'suwet'en, Aboriginal Title and the Rule of Law." 10 June 2020. https://www.firstpeopleslaw.com/public-education/blog/category/wetsuweten.

McKittrick, Katherine. "Plantation Futures." *Small Axe: A Caribbean Journal of Criticism* 17, no. 3/42 (November 2013): 1–15.

McRuer, Robert, and Abby Wilkerson. *Desiring Disability: Queer Theory Meets Disability Studies.* Special issue of *GLQ: A Journal of Lesbian and Gay Studies* 9, no. 1–2 (2003).

Michalko, Rod. *The Difference That Disability Makes.* Philadelphia: Temple University Press, 2002.

———. *The Mystery of the Eye and the Shadow of Blindness.* Toronto: University of Toronto Press, 1998.

———. *The Two in One: Walking with Smokie, Walking with Blindness.* Philadelphia: Temple University Press, 1999.

Million, Dian. *Therapeutic Nation: Healing in an Age of Indigenous Human Rights.* Tucson: University of Arizona Press, 2013.

Mitchell, David. "Narrative Prosthesis and the Materiality of Metaphor." In *Disability Studies: Enabling the Humanities,* edited by Sharon L. Snyder, Brenda Jo Brueggemann, and Rosemarie Garland-Thomson, 15–29. New York: Modern Languages Association of America, 2002.

Morris, Jenny. *Pride against Prejudice: Transforming Attitudes to Disability.* London: Women's Press, 1991.

Obomsawin, Alanis. *Kanehsatake: 270 Years of Resistance.* National Film Board, 1993. Available at https://www.nfb.ca/film/kanehsatake_270_years_of_resistance/.

Oliver, Mike. *The Politics of Disablement.* London: Macmillan, 1990.

———. *Understanding Disability: From Theory to Practice.* New York: St. Martin's Press. 1996.

Palmater, Pamela. *Warrior Life: Indigenous Resistance and Resurgence.* Halifax and Winnipeg: Fernwood Publishing, 2020.

Parker, Laurence, and Marvin Lynn. "What's Race Got to Do with It? Critical Race Theory's Conflicts with and Connections to Qualitative Research Methodology and Epistemology." *Qualitative Inquiry* 8, no. 1 (2002): 7–22.

Pickens, Therí Alyce. *Black Madness: Mad Blackness.* Durham, NC: Duke University Press, 2019.

———. "Blue Blackness, Black Blueness: Making Sense of Blackness and Disability." *African American Review* 50, no. 2 (2017): 93–103.

Sacks, Harvey. "On Doing 'Being Ordinary.'" In *Structures in Social Action: Studies in Conversational Analysis,* edited by J. Maxwell Atkinson and John Heritage, 413–29. Cambridge: Cambridge University Press, 1984.

Sanders, Clinton. "The Impact of Guide Dogs on the Identity of People with Visual Impairments." *Anthrozoös* 13, no. 3 (2000): 131–39.

———. *Understanding Dogs: Living and Working with Canine Companions.* Philadelphia: Temple University Press, 1999.

Shakespeare, Tom, ed. *The Disability Studies Reader: Social Science Perspectives.* London: Cassell, 1998.

Smith, Dorothy E. *The Everyday World as Problematic: A Feminist Sociology.* Toronto: University of Toronto Press. 1987.

Stiker, Henri-Jacques. *A History of Disability.* Trans. William Sayers. Ann Arbor: University of Michigan Press, 1999.

Taylor, Sunaura. *Beasts of Burden: Animal and Disability Liberation.* New York: The New Press, 2017.

Titchkosky, Tanya. *Disability, Self, and Society.* Toronto: University of Toronto Press, 2003.

———. *The Question of Access: Disability, Space, Meaning.* Toronto: University of Toronto Press, 2011.

Todd, Zoe. "Fish Pluralities: Human-Animal Relations and Sites of Engagement in Paulatuuq, Arctic Canada." *Ètudes Inuit Studies* 38, nos. 1–2 (2014): 217–38.

Vizenor, Gerald. *Manifest Manners: Narratives on Post Indian Survivance.* Lincoln: University of Nebraska Press, 1999.

Wynter, Sylvia. "On How We Mistook the Map for the Territory, and Reimprisoned Ourselves in Our Unbearable Wrongness of Being, of Désêtre: Black Studies toward the Human Project." In *A Companion to African American Studies,* edited by Lewis Gordon and Jane Anna Gordon, 107–72. New Jersey: Blackwell Publishing, 2006.

———. "Unsettling the Coloniality of Being/Power/Truth/Freedom: Towards the Human, After Man, Its Overrepresentation—An Argument." *CR: The New Centennial Review* 3, no. 3 (2003): 257–337.

Wynter, Sylvia, and Katherine McKittrick. "Unparalleled Catastrophe for Our Species? Or, to Give Humanness a Different Future: Conversations." In *On Being Human as Praxis,* edited by Katherine McKittrick and Sylvia Wynter, 9–89. Durham, NC: Duke University Press, 2015.

Printed in the USA
CPSIA information can be obtained
at www.ICGtesting.com
CBHW030813140224
4305CB00015B/95

9 781772 840339